CONTENTS

Armoured Train at North Walsham
On November 14th 1914, the Railway War Manufacturers sub-committee of the Railway Executive authorised the construction of two armoured train for coastal defence. Each train consisted of: two 30-ton Caledonian Railway boiler-trolleys, converted for use as gun trucks; two 40-ton GWR coal trucks, which were used as infantry vans; and an 0-6-2 side tank loco. Later a locomotive tender was provided to give the extra capacity required for the long patrols which the trains undertook, these patrol areas being on the NBR lines north of Edinburgh, and on the Midland & Great Northern Joint lines, where the picture was taken.
NATIONAL RAILWAY MUSEUM

RAILWAYS AT WAR 1914-1918
ALAN EARNSHAW

ISBN 0-906899-39-7   FIRST PUBLISHED 1990

No part of this publication may be reproduced in any form or by any means without the prior written permission of the publishers.

© TEXT: Dr. Alan Earnshaw
PHOTOGRAPHS: As credited.

DESIGNED BY
BARNABUS DESIGN & PRINT . TRURO . CORNWALL
TYPESET BY
TYPESTYLE · TRURO · CORNWALL
PRINTED BY
CENTURY LITHO · PENRYN · CORNWALL
BOUND BY
BOOTHS BOOKBINDERS · PENRYN · CORNWALL
PUBLISHED BY

ATLANTIC TRANSPORT PUBLISHERS
TREVITHICK HOUSE · WEST END
PENRYN · CORNWALL TR10 8HE

Front cover, top: *A LNWR 0-6-0 Coal Engine No. 3412 working on supply duties near Velu. Of the 85 members of this class which were supplied to the ROD, over half of them were never to return. Some were lost in the war, but many others were transferred to work in Egypt as they were un-suited to the strenuous working conditions in France. The small tender capacity was their biggest weakness, but it is debatable whether engines dating from the 1880s were suitable for despatch overseas at all.*
IMPERIAL WAR MUSEUM

Front cover, bottom: *More normally associated with race-course traffic, the small station at the Curragh plays host to the Manchester Regiment in August 1914. The two troop trains are an interesting example of the mixed stock trains used in the Mobilisation, being formed up from 4-wheel, 6-wheel and bogie coaches, along with horse (cattle) vans and goods vehicles for stores.*
BY KIND PERMISSION OF THE MANCHESTER REGIMENT COURTESY OF THE MUSEUMS OF MANCHESTER

Rear cover, top: *Two products of the war: one of the 'tanks' which changed the course of warfare is seen on one of the rail vehicles specially designed to carry them. After the war these 'Rectank' wagons were used for a variety of purposes in addition to that of carrying armoured fighting vehicles.* NATIONAL RAILWAY MUSEUM

Rear cover, bottom: *From 1915 onwards the railway workshops played an increasingly important role in the manufacture of munitions and instruments of war. Amidst the part-built locomotives at Horwich in 1917 a howitzer awaits despatch to the battlefields.* NATIONAL RAILWAY MUSEUM

Introduction

Until the release of the series, Britain's Railways At War, the subject of how our nation's railways coped in times of national emergency had been scantily covered in recent years. Indeed the first volume only touched the surface of the subject, presenting glimpses of our railways in the period 1939-45. Though there is much still to be said about World War II, I felt that this present volume should provide a similar introduction to the First World War.

None of these books are designed to glorify war, and those who seek such entertainment perhaps need read no further. Because, from whatever standpoint you take, war is a dirty, dreadful business. It manifests brutality in otherwise normal men, results in untold squalor, suffering and death, and in its wake leaves widows, orphans, and abject misery. Nevertheless it is an evocative subject, and one which deserves covering in all its aspects – if only to show mankind the futility of it all. From our standpoint we will look at how the railways were organised for, and coped with war service. Retrospectively, many noted historians have said that 'August 1914 was the month the world went mad'. Indeed, since that time, the world has seen little peace, and it can be said that these events were a major turning point in the history of mankind. True, there had been serious wars before 1914-18, but never had any embroiled the whole of the civilised world, and involved such modern weaponry as to claim 16 million lives.

It is therefore necessary to briefly summarise the political situation that caused the Great War, and note the major events which led to the British involvement. The origins can be traced back to the Franco-Prussian War of 1870, where Germany emerged as victors and under Bismark began to enjoy national prosperity. In turn this lead to growth of German socialism, and although Bismark tried to suppress the Social Democratic Party, it eventually swept to power in the national elections of November 1912. As early as 1909 Winston Churchill, had drawn attention to the growing tension in Germany, by stating 'Will the tension be relieved by moderation, or snapped by calculated violence?' He also envisaged that any such 'violence' may take the form of an adventure outside Germany,

Within weeks of the declaration of war, almost every bill-board and hoarding in the land displayed posters calling men to arms. It was no different on railway advertising displays, as testified by the 10 recruiting banners on display at Liverpool in December 1914.
NATIONAL RAILWAY MUSEUM

which might serve to distract Germans from their troubles at home.

Meanwhile, the Austro-Hungarian Empire was in constant danger of disintegration. The ruling Habsburg-Magyar dual dynasty was still in power, but the Empire was threatened by so many schisms from within that there seemed the ever present threat of revolution. National-Socialists were in open alliance with Russia, and combined with disaffected Serbs, Slavs, and Moravians, the minority groups almost equalled the strength of the ruling powers. The only thing which prevented full-scale anarchy was the fact these dissident groups had not yet sufficiently settled their individual differences to pose a serious threat.

In Turkey, the situation was somewhat different, for their national aim was one of conquest and the creation of a Pan-Turkish Empire. Which could only be accomplished by removing what the Turks called the 'Russian despotism' in the surrounding Balkan nations. This aspiration was almost realised by the Russian Revolution of 1905, which set not only that country, but the whole of Europe into tumult. International monetary aid helped the Tsar recover his position, but the situation was still critical. In France the situation was also tense, and though island Britain remained aloof from these entanglements, it too was pre-occupied with civil unrest in the case of the Irish question.

The strange climax to these troubles began on June 14th 1914, in a time when at last peace seemed more assured. That day was the 14th wedding anniversary of Archduke Franz Ferdinand heir apparent to the Austro-Hungarian throne. As his wife Sophie Chotek was a mere countess, many regarded her as a poor choice, and she was never allowed to sit by his side on public occasions. However, as Inspector General of the Army, he was allowed to have his wife with him when he was acting in an official capacity at military reviews. So in desiring to spend his anniversary with his wife, he arranged to inspect his army in Bosnia. The review was to be held in the capital Sarajevo, but events of that day were to set the whole world ablaze. An assassination attempt had been plotted by six disaffected students from a local grammar school, aided and abetted by a Serb secret society who supplied the boys with crude weapons. During the drive into Sarajevo a bomb was thrown, and the infuriated Franz Ferdinand decided to drive straight out of the town. In the confusion one of the boys, Cavrilo Princip, stepped on the running board of the stationary car and shot the Royal couple dead.

Many historians think this was the excuse the world powers had been seeking for so long, yet few of the military leaders wanted war, as they recognised it would cause an un-precedent holocaust. Indeed the Austrians had experienced serious trouble with the Serbs before, and had always been able to subdue them. Following Sarajevo they turned to their German allies for advice, who suggested that they take a firm hand with Serbia. The Austrians were reluctant to do anything hasty, but on July 23rd, they sent the Serbian Government an ultimatum designed to humiliate it. The terms were accepted by the Serbs, but not Russia who proclaimed itself 'Protector of the Balkan States'. They stepped in, and threatened to mobilise against the Austro-Hungarian Empire. Such was the threat and counter-threat of European politics at that time, that it was anticipated that this would cause the respective parties to shrink back and thus ensure peace.

None of this bluff and bravado took into account what would actually happen if one country did mobilise, thus setting the long-prepared plans into motion. Previously mobilisation had been a long, drawn-out affair, but this was all changed to a matter of days by the involvement of the railways. In A. J. P. Taylor's book 'The First World War', it states that World War One was '. . . the unexpected climax to the railway age', and further cites the escalation on the railways by stating, 'Railway timetables, cannot be improvised. Once started, the wagons and carriages must roll remorselessly and inevitably forward to their predestined goal.' Basically, this is a simplistic view of the railway-based invasion plans which each country had drawn up in the latter part of the 19th century. Though these plans involved huge numbers of men, they could have been cancelled in the early stages, but once fully mobilised, war was almost inevitable, the common saying of 1912-4 was 'Mobilisation means War'.

Perhaps the greatest exponent of the concept was Schlieffen, Chief of the German General Staff from 1862 to 1906. He recognised that Germany could not possibly engage against France and Russia at the same time, so his grand plan called for the first advance to be against France. Germany estimated that the Russian mobilisation was sure to be slower than the French, and the Schlieffen plan was based on quick action in penetrating the enemy's defence. The railways were his means of accomplishing this and all the build-up was along the western border, unfortunately these plans were unexpectedly upset when the Russians mobilised in late July. On the 31st, Germany demanded their demobilisation within twelve hours or they would declare war, the Russians refused and hostilities began on August 1st. Two days later Germany declared war of France and demanded free passage for its troops through Belgium. The Belgians refused and were invaded, an action which eventually brought Britain into the war on August 5th.

All over Europe armies and reserve forces were rolling up to their allotted stations, and away went the trains to their pre-arranged destinations: taking with them an estimated six million men, who were deposited on the various sides of the battle-fields. In the few short pages of this second volume we can not possibly present a detailed history of all the railway events of 1914-18, but we hope that it will provide a fascinating over-view of the role played by Britain's railways.

At a meeting of the War Cabinet in January 1917, instructions were given for the construction of a train-ferry service between England and France. Two English terminals were constructed, one at Richborough and one at Southampton, connecting the ports of Calais and Dunkirk. The service did not start until February 10th 1918, when three identical ferries were commissioned. Each had a main train-deck, which carried four sets of parallel lines, giving a total track length of 1,080 ft. This afforded the carriage of 54 standard wagons or the equivalent in coaches or locomotives. The vessels were twin screw with two sets of triple-expansion engines, and were capable of about 12 knots. They were provided with search-lights, wireless and anti-aircraft/submarine guns. A crew of 65 manned the vessels, but no passengers were carried.
THE TANK MUSEUM

The naval build-up was much slower than the army's, and many historians point to the fact that this was due to perpetual penny-pinching by successive governments. Whether this is an accurate overall picture or not, it is certainly true of the rail facilities connected with our maritime defence. There was a general shortage of the special rail wagons which were required to meet the Navy's unusual demands. As in the case of vehicles for conveying heavy guns: a few 'gun-sets' capable of carrying guns up to 100 tons were available but these were unlikely to be sufficient in a war. In the meanwhile, guns like the 56 ton example seen at Toton in 1906, had to be carried on an improvised 'gun-set' and is mounted on two MR armour-plate wagons (Nos. 116073 and 34842) Traction engine truck D333 and a 10-ton brake van complete the train.
NATIONAL RAILWAY MUSEUM

The engine that came back! Of all the railway equipment despatched to France, provision was made for expendable losses, allowing for enemy action. However, it was understood that the enemy must not be allowed to capture British equipment intact, and if this was likely, the equipment should be destroyed first. This was not the case with a Midland 0-6-0, No. 2717 which was captured by the Germans near Cambrai in 1917. After being put to use on German controlled lines, it was later re-captured and returned to the Midland Railway after the armistice.
NATIONAL RAILWAY MUSEUM

Preparation for War

The abiding memory of most participants in the mobilisation of August 1914, is the role the railways played, and the smooth running of the entire transport operations. What is not so widely known, are the extensive efforts put into the preparation of the mobilisation plans. In railway terms the origins of these could be traced back over fifty years. The American Civil War (1861-5) showed the effectiveness of rail transport in modern warfare, and it was in the Prussian State of Germany that there came the first planned system for the utilisation of railways in wartime. The idea spread through Europe, and soon each country had evolved plans for, if not actually formed, strategical railway troops. The basic concept was the formation of a construction corps, and a railway reserve. These trained railwaymen and engineers would follow the advancing army, taking control of, repairing, and operating captured railway systems to support further military advances.

In England the concept had been advanced by the Duke of Wellington as early as 1845, but it was not until 1860 that there came the proposal to form a railway reserve to act in support of coastal defences in the time of national emergency. Various reports were studied, but that by Charles Manby FRS was accepted, and in January 1865 the Engineer & Railway Volunteer Staff Corps was formed. Its purpose 'to direct the skilled labour and of railway transport to the purposes of national defence, and for the preparing, in time of peace, a system on which duties should be conducted'. It is interesting to note that such duties were strictly confined to the British Isles, and unlike all the other European countries, Britain did not envisage the need for 'occupationary railway troops'. This largely stemmed from the fact that Britain was an island, and it had no adjoining country which it might be forced to occupy. The result of this was to dog the Railway Reserve for

---

As the stern realities of the conflict in France became realised in the autumn of 1914, the public hope that 'the war would be over by Christmas' gradually disappeared. It was to be a war of attrition, and the winning of it would largely depend on the side with the best organisation for getting men and munitions to the Front. In February 1915 Lord Kitchener enlisted the assistance of the NER's Mr. Eric C. Geddes in speeding up the movement of munitions and other vital materials. Then on October 7th 1916 he was made Director-General of Military Railways and Deputy Quartermaster General (Transport), yet within just two weeks he was also appointed as Inspector General of Transport to the British Armies in France. In order for him to inspect the facilities under his control, a train of eight 6-wheeled coaches was placed at his disposal. The train is pictured here with an NER 2-4-2T No. 205, the baggage and store vans are marshalled at the front.

NATIONAL RAILWAY MUSEUM

---

many years, and ensured that (a) it was only ever a numerically small reserve, and (b) that Government spending was proportionately low.

The Corps was purely voluntary (until it became part of the Territorial Reserve 1907) and was initially staffed only by officers. Its members were contractors, civil engineers, railway and dock managers, and in some instances members of the Board of Trade. But in an emergency, the Corps figured it could rely on 12,000 to 20,000 men, mostly navvies. Its main work was drawing up the mobilisation timetables, by which the railways would speed men to the defence of the realm. Though establishing the Corps was a major step, the Government felt it needed to be able to control and coordinate the various railway, naval and military needs of a country at war. Therefore in 1896, the War Office created the Army Railway Council, which was comprised of two representatives of the Quarter-master General, six railway managers (four from England and one each from Ireland and Scotland), two members of the Corps, one BoT Inspector, one Mobilisation Officer, and two officers from the Admiralty.

The council's objectives were: (1) generally advise the Secretary of State for War on railway matters; (2) to arrange with all railway companies a detailed scheme in the event of mobilisation; (3) settle the number and composition of trains required to effect same; (4) to determine the best ways of communicating War Office needs to and from the railway companies; (5) to

All manner of railway facilities were to be put at the disposal of the military, including the Cottage Hospital at the L&YR's Horwich Works, opened in 1895. A group of convalescing servicemen are pictured here with the sister in 1915, but note the 'ghetto-blaster' in the corner as evidence that even back then, hospital wards were not altogether the strict, quiet places we might imagine.
NATIONAL RAILWAY MUSEUM

determine the key stations where Railway Staff Officers would be located, and how they could act as intermediaries between the railways and the War Office; (6) to determine where extra sidings, platforms and loading facilities would be needed. The results of the council's objectives were not immediately evident, and indeed the full council only met four times between 1897 and 1910, but things were moving quietly ahead. The South African War and the Boxer Rebellion in China prompted the Government to look more closely at the needs of its railways in war, and in 1903 the name of the council was changed to War Railway Council – a title more in keeping with the wishes of the Lords of the Admiralty.

In 1903 the work of mobilisation timetables was taken up afresh, and although the various military powers were reluctant to supply such 'secret' data, the railway companies could not work without it. The debate was long and hard, but suffice it to say, that by compromise the information was supplied and the work was entrusted to a select few timetable experts. This mammoth task was undertaken with little or no remuneration, and the strain imposed by the work led to the early death of one noted expert. Meanwhile, a more strenuous debate went on about the formation of a pool of 4ft 8 1/2in gauge locomotives, rolling stock and workers, which the Council expected the railway companies to supply in the times of emergency overseas. The companies were reluctant to do this without sufficient compensation, but the Government took the view that its various colonial governments had agreed to supply 3ft 6in gauge stock at only nominal costs, and the companies should do likewise. There the matter remained dead-locked, but as war drew near the situation was amicably resolved as we will see later. Meanwhile on the 'home front', preparations went ahead – ostensibly for National Defence, though the far-sighted could see the developing role of the railways in times of aggression. In 1911 the country was divided into Commands, and for each area command, a secretary railway company was appointed to coordinate the needs of the military. These were:-

Eastern Command – South Eastern & Chatham;

Southern Command – London & South Western;

Western Command – LNWR;

North Command – North Eastern;

Scottish Command – North British;

Irish Command – Great Northern of Ireland.

Under the command system the mobilisation, which had previously been a relatively small matter, became an exceedingly serious concern.

From here-on in, the control of the railways in wartime assumed even greater significance, especially in view of the critical developments in international politics in 1911. It was yet to be resolved how the Government could control the railways in time of war, ensuring both the needs of the civil population and the demands of the War Office. Basically it had two options: (1) to employ section 16 of the Regulation of the Forces Act (1871), which would allow it to take over the complete running of the railways, as though under state control through military law; or, (2) to employ the National Defence Act of 1888, allowing the Government to demand individual companies to comply with its needs and wishes in time of emergency. Initially the latter Act seemed the most expedient, and in general, railway managers were extremely apprehensive about letting the state take control of the railways. Unfortunately, the second Act did not allow for any harmonious development of national railway services which would be needed in times of war. Indeed, the Government had very serious grounds for believing that delays would be occasioned to vital military traffic where one railway system met with another.

The real salvation finally came in a totally unexpected form, from a group which had been established to devise the strategy for provisioning London and the south east during times of war with continental Europe. This group was a sub-committee of the War Railway Council, and comprised of the general managers of the LNWR, GWR, LSWR, GNR, GCR and Midland. Under the chairmanship of Frank Ree (LNWR), the committee formulated its specified objectives, but added three recommendations which would at last resolve the issues of who controlled the railway when war eventually broke out. These were:- (1) Adoption of the 1871 Act,

The vast camp of the Lancashire Fusiliers near Turton & Edgeworth station, on the Bolton-Blackburn line in 1914. In the foreground is a special gun-powder train, complete with armed guard, possibly indicating its role as an ammunition train. All the vans are L&YR dia. 3 conversions, with the roof-doors filled in. Their cleanliness and immaculate paint-work suggests an ex-works condition. The vehicles are marked return empty to Gathurst *where a chemical/explosive works had long been established.*
B. C. LANE COLLECTION

bringing all railways and tramways under a single authority; (2) creation of a permanent body of railway managers to ensure the operation of the railways when they passed under state control; and (3) the creation of a consultative body which would bring together representatives of the railways and state departments to a mutual benefit.

At last everyone who mattered agreed, and the Railway Executive Committee was eventually formed at a meeting of the BoT on November 5th 1912. Its members were F. Ree (LNWR and acting chairman), H. A. Walker (LSWR and deputy chairman), J. A. F. Aspinall (L&YR), O. R. H. Bury (GNR), A. K. Butterworth (NER), Sir S. Fay (GCR), G. Garnett (MR), D. A. Matheson (CR), and F. Potter (GWR). In January 1913, Bury resigned and was replaced by the GNR's new general manager C. H. Dent. Five months later F. H. Dent of the South Eastern & Chatham was appointed as a representative of the BoT. This committee

served through the last few years of peace, and performed vital functions during the mobilisation exercises of 1913. It was greatly aided in this period by the Communications Board set up under clause 3 of Ree's recommendations, the members of that committee being of such standing in military and political fields that they could almost instantly give approval to any request from the Railway Executive. Interestingly the head of the Board was the Quarter-master General, Sir John Steven Cowans KCB, MVO. Though a military man through and through, he was eminently suited for the position, as he had a great personal interest

in railways and their operation. His father being the noted railway engineer John Cowans, who had worked for George Stephenson before starting his own firm of Cowans, Sheldon & Co. in 1846. So in a state of almost absolute preparation, the railways were ready for the events of August 1914.

Every soldier's nightmare – a Regimental Sergeant Major awaits the new arrivals at Winchester Station in August 1914. The scouts waiting with him were in fact used as messengers, and were not (as might be imagined) under-age recruits!
HAMPSHIRE RECORD OFFICE

State control begins

In reality, the British Government declared war on Germany at 11 pm (London time) on August 4th, which was midnight on the continent. Exactly one hour later the Railway Executive Committee took control of the railways, from its central office in the LNWR buildings at 35, Parliament St. Westminster. Just days before the declaration of war, a private telephone system had been completed, linking the committee's office to those of its regional control centres. These were at the offices of the L&YR in Manchester, the Midland at Derby, and the NER at York. Further links were installed between Parliament St., and the various Government and Military departments. Notice was sent to the railway companies, first by telephone, then by telegram, and later confirmed in writing by an order from the War Office. Therefore as from 00.01 on August 5th, two-thirds of Britain's railway companies came under state control.

Yet, the statement control is misleading for, in the main, it was anything but. The management structures, the administration, and to a large extent the traffic patterns remained, just as they had been in peace-time. What changed were the working arrangements, at least as far as important military and governmental traffic was concerned. Priorities being assigned to this, and imposed in addition to the mobilisation timetables agreed on beforehand by the respective companies. In this regard, some of the mobilisation programmes did seriously affect the normal operations of the individual companies, and in many cases lead to the curtailment and even the cancellation of several services. In some instances, particularly the London connecting lines and those leading to the cross-channel ports, the

Herbert A. Walker, General Manager of the London & South Western Railway, and chairman of the Railway Executive from May 1914 to December 1919. In fact both Ree and Walker were only acting-chairman, for officially the title chairman was vested in the President of the Board of Trade to provide an impartial head to whom inter-company disputes might be referred. Otherwise the acting-chairman held the real authority, and Walker used his to good effect right through the war years.

NATIONAL RAILWAY MUSEUM

As part of the mobilisation large quantities of railway equipment were released for military use on the order of the Railway Executive. On September 12th 1914, a train of 15 L&YR delivery drays is assembled and awaits departure from Newton Heath, Manchester, for Southampton, from where they will be shipped to France. NATIONAL RAILWAY MUSEUM

cuts were quite savage. However elsewhere, despite some delays, it was mostly business as usual.

In all, 130 companies were 'taken over', though 46 were not. Quite how the selection was made is uncertain, but obviously reference was made to those lines which had important strategic or economic importance. In such cases, the size of the undertaking was immaterial, as was the case with the small lines which provided useful connections between the major railways. Yet there were several anomalies. Many dock railway systems were taken over, but others like those at Felixstowe, the Manchester Ship Canal and Milford Haven were not. It was the same with the light mineral railways: for example, why exclude the Talyllyn, when the Festiniog was taken under the Executive's control?

Another apparent anomaly, the Killin Railway

from Loch Tay, is more easily understood, when one considers the vital timber traffic which originated on it. Even so, it is inconceivable to think that the little Easingwold Railway, with just one tank loco, four coaches and ten trucks, could have had any possible military value to the state. By contrast, the Government grants provided to construct the Wick & Lybster (£25,000) and the Dornoch (£14,945) railways, now became apparent with the War Office revealing that they had supported construction of these lines. Though they were ostensibly constructed to serve local fishing communities, we may ask, had they actually been seen as the most expedient way of protecting those parts of the Scottish Coast? The Admiralty had long known of a theoretical plan to invade the remote coast, somewhere between Dornoch Point and Sinclairs Bay in order to cut supply routes to the important naval anchorages in northern Scotland. The construction of these lines reduced that threat, cutting down the isolated area to an acceptable 19 mile section between Helmsdale and Lybster.

It will be recalled that one of the objectives set by the War Railway Council, was to provide for and establish, new lines, connections, sidings and the like. Some of

these will be discussed later, but four major works were immediately ordered by the Executive. All of these provided physical connections between other railways, and all were installed for strategic military reasons, primarily related to defence matters. The first was the double junction at Gospel Oak, joining the Tottenham & Hampstead Junction Railway and the LNWR; providing a through route between the LNWR and the GER and the London Tilbury and Southend section of the Midland Railway. Second, was another line off the T&HJR, allowing for a single track connection from near Crouch Station, to the GNR at Harringay. Next came a 'defensive link' between the Midland and GNR lines at Peterborough, but after little or no use, it was removed after the war. Finally, a 700 yd long link was provided between Whetstone on the GCR main line, and Blaby on the LNWR's South Leicester line.

Thus it came to be, that but for a few exceptions, all the railways of Britain could be regarded as a single system at the outbreak of war; inasmuch as they allowed the through passage of trains anywhere between Thurso and Penzance, or Margate and the Kyle of Localsh, all the separate and individual companies were working towards a common objective!

9

By contrast a number of lines carrying vital traffic were not taken into control, as for example, the Ravenglass Railway on the Cumberland coast. This line carried a considerable amount of iron-ore traffic in the pre-war years, most of which was consigned to steel works along the coast. It would almost certainly have been taken over as a controlled line, but for the fact that it had been closed since the depression of 1908. It re-opened after war was declared and despite its diminutive gauge, it continued to provide a vital link between the mines and quarries of Eskdale and the Furness Railway's coastal line between Barrow and Whitehaven.
RAVENGLASS & ESKDALE RAILWAY CO.

When the list of state controlled railways was drawn up, there were a few unusual inclusions amongst which was the little Easingwold Railway. From its junction with NER main line at Alne the little branch ambled into a rural back-water. Unless one considers the agricultural produce shipped along the branch, it is hard to imagine what strategic value the line could hold for the Executive Committee. After the war it was returned to private ownership, but what effect state control had on the company is difficult to say. In this post-war view, the company's solitary locomotive is seen at Easingwold with an ex-NER 6-wheeled coach.
T. J. EDGINGTON COLLECTION

The Mobilisation

So far as the mobilisation went, the Admiralty held a test run for its reserve forces on July 12-14th as the likelihood of war drew ever closer. In this regard several ships put to sea, and the demobilisation of these Naval Reservists was not fully completed before war was declared. Elsewhere, the Army Reservists, Militia, and the Territorials were called up on July 26th for the first of the annual training camps. The second series of camps were to commence on Sunday August 3rd, a problem which was compounded, by the fact that the Navy had decided to call up all its remaining reservists on the 2nd which fact alone required the running of 239 special trains. However, the railway companies foresaw immense difficulties with this, as civilian traffic would also peak on August 2nd because of the annual holidays. Feeling they would be unable to manage if war was declared that weekend, the Railway Executive asked the War Office to defer the second series of training camps, but surprisingly the Secretary of State refused.

It was a situation which had been unforseen in all the peace-time planning, and one which threatened to throw the whole mobilisation programme into chaos. By the Sunday morning, conditions on the continent were so grave, that many units arriving at stations to go away to camp, were turned back to their 'drill halls' on an order from the Secretary of State for War. Those en-route were often halted in mid-journey, and their trains turned back, others found that no sooner had they arrived at their camp, than they were sent home again. In addition to this, the recall of those who had been at camp since July 26th, imposed an immense strain on the railways that Sunday. For example, the little Cambrian Railway had to suddenly find 27 trains to transport 9,000 men from the Welsh Territorial camps at Aberystwyth and Portmadoc on what was their busiest weekend of the year. Down in the south, the tiny station at Amesbury on the L&SWR handled no less than 38 trains, sent to convey the forces of the Home Counties Brigade back home.

The general mobilisation came into effect from 00.01 on August 5th, coinciding with the state control of the railways. The programme of Mobilisation Days began at the same time, August 5th being day one. To avoid congestion at stations, each unit had an assembly day and time, therefore those with the order MOB+02-11 reported to their allotted railway stations at 11 am on the second day (ie the 6th) and so on. The mobilisation lasted for 14 days and took no special account of August 10th and 17th which were Sundays, but treated as normal working days. Each group was given a priority order in the mobilisation scheme, 1st) Territorials, 2nd) the Reservists, 3rd)

Two views of 'Calling men to the colours' in Dewsbury; the first is taken outside the Town Hall, with troops assembled in the square adjacent to the L&YR station. The curiously worded slogan on the buildings refers to the enlistment target set by the Town Council, which promised 2,000 men for the army. When this photograph was taken on August 19th 1914, the number of recruits had apparently reached one quarter of the target.

After parading in the town, the men were marched to one of Dewsbury's three passenger stations. They are seen here waiting to depart from the elevated island platform of Dewsbury GNR, many will be wearing uniforms made from woolen cloth produced in the town. Indeed, some may even be among the 1,287 textile workers who were later recalled from the army to work in the industry. The vast majority never returned, for these 'Pals' battalions suffered some of the heaviest casualties of the war.

BOTH KIRKLEES MUSEUMS & LIBRARIES

Special Reservists (the militia), 4th) Horses for the regular army. During the mobilisation period the number of trains run was staggering, over 632 originated on the GWR alone, whilst the LNWR supplied 550.

Initially, it has been planned for priority in all cases to be given to the six infantry and one cavalry divisions which had been formed to make the British Expeditionary Force. Pre-war plans had envisaged the embarkation of this Force on the same day as war was declared, but for various reasons this did not begin until August 9th. This was partly due to the concurrent demands placed on the Railway Executive by different Government departments, and the amended orders for extra trains to be supplied to the different Area Commands.

Therefore it was essential to re-model the mobilisation timetables, and the BEF embarkation was amended to commence MOB+5. This did not greatly disrupt events, and thanks to the smoothness of pre-war planning, the required changes were easily made. The first BEF train arrived at Southampton at 8.48 am August 9th, with the last arriving there at 6 pm on August 17th. Altogether 334 trains ran, carrying the initial force of 68,847 officers and men, 21,523 horses, 166 field guns, 2,446 vehicles, 1,368 bicycles, and 2,550 tons of stores. When the reinforcement programme had been completed by August 31st, some 670 trains

had run in total, with commensurate increases in the figures quoted above.

Again the information concerning the mobilisation and the despatch of troops to France is so great, it is impossible to recount it all. Suffice it to say, the railway played a supremely important role, as testified to by the comments of Secretary of War,. Lord Kitchener, in an address to the House of Lords on August 25th:-

'The railway companies, in the all-important matter of transport facilities, have more than justified the complete confidence reposed in them by the War Office, all grades of railway services having laboured with untiring energy and patience.'

Troop Trains

Great as the mobilisation was, it might be regarded as just the tip of the iceberg. Whereas the numbers of troops carried in the initial period could be counted in tens of thousands, those which followed were numbered in millions. Additionally, whilst those moved under the mobilisation followed a pre-ordained plan, the later troop traffic was subject to different arrangements. Apart from a short period at the end of 1914, all subsequent troop movements were coordinated by the Army Area Commands which we discussed in the introduction.

It will be recalled that to each Command was appointed a secretary railway company, through which all railway matters were handled. This system remained basically un-altered throughout the war, although in 1915 the South Eastern & Chatham company was superseded by the LNWR as the secretary company for the Eastern Command. This was due to the heavy administrative duties already engaged in by the SE&CR, who were inundated with work pertaining to the lines supplying the channel-ports. On the other hand, the much larger LNWR were able to absorb the work in spite of already acting as secretary company to the Western Area Command.

The work of these secretary companies was most interesting, and largely involved the complete reversal of normal railway administrative practice: ie, the working of train routes and timetables from the destination backwards! Though quite confusing, it was an essential requirement for the War Office, who had to have troops at certain embarkation ports at a specified time in order for them and their baggage to be loaded onto the correct ships. Therefore an Area Command would be issued with the War Office directive that A, B and C battalions of X regiment, embark Folkestone at such and such a time. This command would be addressed to the secretary company, along with a note of what was to be carried. Firstly the company would plan what stock was needed, ie: the number of first-class coaches for officers, the seating accommodation for NCOs and enlisted men, cattle trucks for horses, box vans for stores, and open wagons of artillery, vehicles etc. It would then ascertain if the train could be worked through to its destination by a single locomotive and crew, or if it would have to be handed on to another company en-route.

If the train was to be worked through to its destination as a single unit, a number of important issues had first to be resolved. Most importantly, could the stock of the originating company comply with the loading gauge of the receiving railway, and any others it might pass through on its journey? Likewise, would the locomotives assigned to the task be within any axle-loading restrictions on the lines on which it would travel? Both of these points were especially critical in East Anglia, Northern Scotland and certain parts of Wales. Further, it was essential that pilot drivers were available when a through train reached the junction with another company, for it was impractical to send men along lines of which they could not possibly have any route knowledge. Arrangements would have to be made in

---

The 3rd Royal Fusiliers await their troop train at Hook Station on August 20th 1914. They are pictured with the boy scouts who had acted as runners for the soldiers whilst they were camped in Hampshire, until the regiment was shipped out to France. Note the lady seated centre, and the railway staff looking on.
HAMPSHIRE RECORD OFFICE

respect of watering and coaling the locomotive, in addition to food or lodging for the train crew if they were away from their home shed over a specified length of time. Finally, it had to be seen if there could be any counter-balancing traffic, which would obviate the wasteful, empty return workings. Such considerations all weighed heavily against the system of through trains, but a great many were run for expediency's sake. Indeed as the war progressed, many drivers became so adept at taking their charges over 'foreign' systems, they were able to do this without pilots.

Generally speaking, the vast majority of crews handed over trains at the inter-company boundaries, where locomotives of that system would take over. Whilst this reduced the number of 'foreign' locos seen on some lines, the same could not be said of coaching and goods stock. For example, one photograph submitted for this book (though not used because of its poor quality) showed Highland Railway passenger stock at Avonmouth Docks. Another view presented GCR coaches in Inverness. Obviously the secretary companies still had to be mindful of the various loading gauge restrictions and the need for counter-balancing but, by careful routing, most trains were able to work all the way to their destination. This minimised the waste of time involved in

Arriving at Folkestone, Soldiers from an un-identified regiment arrive at the port in 1917. The picture presents a fascinating view of the docks and railways during a period when access to the area was actively restricted. Note the dredger which was kept in continuous employment to allow deep-draughted vessels access to the wharves.
NATIONAL RAILWAY MUSEUM

threw an immense burden on the small staff employed in each secretary section; though in reality they were assisted by the Military Railway Staff in each of the companies they worked with. The staff of these military sections was usually around 15 in number; regardless of the size of the particular concern, the maximum rarely exceeded 22. For example the tiny Taff Vale employed as

many men in this duty as did its mighty neighbour the GWR. Each company worked its 'military' department in the way best suited to its own peculiar needs and according to how it interpreted the Railway Executive's orders, but most followed a fairly standard pattern. Therefore, men in the Great North of Scotland Railway, could easily communicate with their counterparts at the Cheshire Lines Committee and so on.

These Military Staffs did immensely valuable liaison work between the railway and the army, and were often called upon to sort out some very awkward situations. They were, so to speak, at the sharp end of the stick, a stick prodded with considerable ferocity by certain military commanders intent on having their own wishes complied with. This largely came from a general misconception of the meaning 'state control of railways' by many officers who believed the railway companies were under martial law. Therefore, local commanders often held the view that railways in *their* district were under *their* command. It therefore irked

Later on the same day, Princess Henrietta is embarking troops before departing from Folkestone. The numbers of men boarding the paddle steamer is so large, that a definite list has developed to starboard. To the left of the picture the troop trains which brought the men to the port can be clearly seen.
NATIONAL RAILWAY MUSEUM

detraining and entraining the troops each time they reached the boundary of one system. In this respect, the back-timing of troop trains was even more important than in those instances where they were worked to their destination by a single engine. For example, a train from Glasgow to Southampton might be worked by the CR, then change at Carlisle to the Midland, at Mexborough it would be handed over to the GCR who would take it as far as the GWR at Banbury, from there it would be taken to Basingstoke and the L&SWR. If the train had to be at Southampton by 5 pm, the programme of hand-over times would be worked back, with a fifteen minute buffer on each time to allow for contingencies. Eventually the Caledonian would be given a time at which the Midland would take the train, and after subtracting its journey time, the time for departure from Glasgow would be arrived at.

At first glance, this system apparently

Equipment train at Newton Heath, with 10 army water carts behind L&YR 0-6-0, No. 288. These water carts were part of an order for 35 such vehicles, each with a 118 gallons capacity galvanised tank. Pumping and filtering apparatus was included, and the water was discharged through a series of taps placed on a cross pipe at the end of the cart. The six-wheeled 'Tin-Tab' brake-van is from Wigan shed.

NATIONAL RAILWAY MUSEUM

them considerably, when some upstart had the afrontery to tell them they couldn't have the trains they wanted. In several instances it is reported that local station-masters were put under armed guard for failing to 'do as they were ordered'. It was a difficult situation, and one which called for immense tact. However, the Military Railway Staff had to firmly point out, they were under direct orders from the War Office, and that if General so-and-so wanted a special train to take him and his wife to London, then the General would have to clear it with the Army Area Command. After the first few months of war these problems gradually died down, and from the end of 1915 onwards only the most cordial of relations are recorded.

It was also the duty of these small 'staffs' to prepare, type up, and duplicate all the timetables pertaining to troop movements that originated in their company's area. These documents were often quite extensive and, because of the nature of the trains, highly confidential. Therefore, even the most routine matters dealt with by these departments had to be handled solely by the small number of men employed in them. For example, right from the outbreak of war, it was practice to fix a sticky label in the windows on the front and rear coaches of troop trains. These labels, even though they bore nothing more than the class and number of the train, were classified as secret. It was the duty of the Military Railway Staff to see the labels were affixed to the train windows, and any surplus ones were immediately burnt. As a matter of interest, these labels were printed in red, and had a single letter, below which was printed three digits. The letter signified the class of train, the digits its number on the general orders, therefore X 123 would be British Expeditionary Force, train No. 123.

Finally, it might be mentioned that the workers employed in connection with these military duties enjoyed a considerable degree of power. For, instance they could comandeer motor vehicles, omnibuses and taxis; they could take over trains on behalf of the executive; and even turf out passengers, travelling on other trains to make way for important journeys by military or naval personnel. Their offices were never closed, being open 24 hours a day, seven days a week. The department's telephones were always continually manned (usually by an operator loaned from the General Post Office), and a motorbike was available for urgent despatches. Thereby, the railway companies were always accessible for any orders which they might be given by the Area Commands concerning troop movements, or any other instructions which might be sent from either the secretary company, or the Railway Executive.

The strangest of all troop trains, a wind-powered inspection cart on the Spurn Point Military Railway. The line itself was built in connection with the Humber Estuary Defence Scheme, and manned by the Royal Engineers. Few photographs of this railway have survived, and this view presents a rare example on a rare line – if any reader has other photographs, both the author and the Hull museums would dearly like to hear about them.

CITY OF KINGSTON UPON HULL, MUSEUMS & ART GALLERIES

Civilian Traffic & Travel Restrictions

Initially, both the press and the railway companies presented the facade that, but for some minor inconveniences, it was to be business as usual. Indeed, had not the war been so prolonged, along with the demand for the release of men and locomotives for service in France, then it may well have been possible to keep up this pretence. During the 14 days of the mobilisation, there were (as might be expected) numerous delays and cancellations to services. This coincided with the main holiday period of 1914, but even so the general public were not overly inconvenienced by it all. The suspension of cheap travel and certain excursion tickets was lifted as early as August 22nd, and many who had been prevented from holidaying earlier that month took the opportunity to travel on the last weekend of August. For example the Down Cornish Riviera ran in no less than 18 parts that Saturday. In fact, if anything, civilian traffic increased throughout the autumn, and this without taking into account people who were using the trains in connection with matters related to the war: ie, Munitions Workers, troops on leave, etc.

By the start of 1915, the reduction in manpower due to the numbers flocking to 'the colours' was beginning to affect the railway companies, but few realised that they were witnessing the greatest war in history unfold. Those at home now found themselves with more and more money to spend, largely due to the increased output in the manufacturing industries. Record wages, and in many cases reduced hours, allowed certain sections of the community more freedom to travel. Joy-riding increased, but along with it, so did the numbers of troop trains, coal trains, and military traffic, a problem compounded by the transfer of virtually all the East Coast shipping traffic on to the railways. The worsening situation was referred to the C14 committee of the Railway Executive, made up from 24 Superintendents of the Line. In meetings held at the Lancashire & Yorkshire Rly's offices in Great College Street, Westminster, various proposals were made for restricting passenger travel, and where possible discouraging it – especially joy-riding. First

King George V and Queen Mary arrive at Dewsbury LNWR station to inspect the various textile mills and clothing factories in the Heavy Woollen District which were involved in uniform manufacturing. Mill workers were given a days holiday, all except those in the factories where the Royal couple were to visit.
KIRKLEES MUSEUMS & LIBRARIES

of these resulted in the withdrawal of 180 competitive trains, all of which duplicated services on other routes. This was followed by the suspension of cheap tickets etc, though once again there were many groups and classes who could still claim travel at reduced rates. These schemes had no appreciable affect, and so, on the Monday before Easter, the availability of the remaining cheap-travel classes was further reduced. Easter came and went, and with it an overall increase of 30% in passenger traffic. In summer the increase was even greater, and almost equalled the record summer of 1913.

The hard-pressed South Eastern & Chatham was faced with an impossible situation, which it addressed later in 1915 by closing several halts and small stations – a move followed by the Midland, Highland and Great Northern railways. The GER tried to follow suit and announced the proposed closure of no fewer than nineteen stations;

the uproar which followed succeeded in reducing the number to fourteen. A further method was seen to increase the capacity of trains, and although an unpalatable measure, January 1916 saw the wide scale withdrawal of restaurant and sleeping car services on many lines in the south. In April the LNWR followed suit on the west coast route, and to prevent them gaining an unfair advantage, this was matched by those companies on the East Coast lines. In May, tourist tickets were suspended, ostensibly for the summer, but in September the order was confirmed for the duration of the war. Notwithstanding all these various reductions in cheap fares, numbers of trains, lack of buffet facilities etc, traffic receipts were considerably higher that Easter. So, to discourage any similar occurrence at Whitsuntide, a Royal Proclamation was made postponing the bank holiday until August 8th, when it would be added to the August Bank Holiday. Traffic on the railways was even greater, as many who had previously booked Whitsun holidays were unable or unwilling to cancel them. The Government, now fearful of the demands on the railways that summer, decided to cancel the August holidays indefinitely, and asked people to stay at home – fat chance! In two days alone, the L&YR handled over 1,000 trains at its stations in Blackpool and Fleetwood, whilst the LB&SCR ran its principal Brighton express in 21 parts. It

seemed, no matter what restrictions were imposed, the public had worked hard for the war effort and earned a holiday which they were jolly well going to have!

This was concurrent with the increasing strain imposed by military traffic on the railways, and the demands of the War Office and Ministry of Munitions for yet more men and locomotives to be released for service in France. The Ministry said it would accept no less than 370 freight engines by the end of the year, a quantity which it was impossible to release with the high level of traffic on the railways at home. At the same time, the Ministry of Munitions compounded the problem, by making it even more difficult for the companies to get the vital raw materials needed by the railway workshops to repair 'failed' locomotives. In September, the Executive announced the number of locomotives awaiting repairs or major overhaul was no less than 476. If 'the powers that be' had been possessed with any sense, they would have seen the solution to both the overseas and home problems sitting on rusted sidings around

the various workshops and engine sheds. True, the types of these 'dead' locos were not what may have been needed for France, but by various juggling acts the railways could almost have instantly supplied what was required. However, it was not to be, and the repair and renewal programme was badly hampered by this fact.

Faced with this stone-wall approach, the Railway Executive had no option but to ask its C14 Superintendent's Committee to look at further ways of achieving travel restrictions which would allow the release of men and machines for France. It came out heavily against the introduction of travel permits, and instead proposed a system of cuts and restrictions that makes

Dr. Beeching look like Santa Claus. How a group of such dedicated railway operators could make these decisions is today beyond comprehension, for in hindsight so many of these 'cuts' left the railways with a legacy from which some lines never recovered. Take for example the little Brampton Town branch of the NER in Cumberland; it was closed on the order of the Executive, despite the fact that over 500 workers were daily using it to travel to the munition works at Gretna and Longtown. The branch re-opened after the war, but like so many others, its patronage had been forced on to bus or tram services, and within a few years it was closed once again – permanently.

It was not only stations and branches

As early as February 1915, the Railway Executive Committee recognised that a shortage of good quality steam coal would ensue if the war became a protracted affair. In March the committee ordered the railway companies to lay in reserve stocks, and by April coal orders from the 12 larger companies had increased by 25%. Coal stacked for emergency use at the GER's Stratford depot, is seen arrayed in superbly built stacks, the art of which owes much to dry-stone walling techniques.
NATIONAL RAILWAY MUSEUM

which were closed, but whole lines of track were ripped up and shipped off to France: sacrificed to the all-important *god* of munitions for the front. In addition to such closures, fares were increased by a hefty 50% and nearly all forms of concessionary travel were abolished in an attempt to discourage public use of the trains. Yet, who at the same time was giving concessionary tickets to its workers, encouraging them to travel home, to the seaside, or just to visit friends? Yes, none other than the Ministry of Munitions!

In order to accomplish these savage cuts, the Board of Trade had to seek powers under the Defence of the Realm Act in order to avoid the legal, technical and contractual obligations which it would have been faced with under pending legislation. There was an understandable up-roar, and Questions were asked in parliament to which the Minister of Munitions replied:-

' The Government is satisfied it can look confidently to the public cheerfully to put up with the restrictions.'

The public didn't, but there was less cheering news to follow. Personal luggage, and luggage sent in advance was limited to

a maximum weight of 100 lbs (250 lbs for an officer in uniform). Express trains were decelerated and made to stop at intermediate stations, and many stopping trains were reduced. Mixed trains, that is to say made up of passenger and freight stock, were to be introduced, despite the fact that this practice had long been condemned by the Accident Inspectors of the BoT. The number of closed stations was increased to over 400, whilst the majority of those remaining open were closed from 10 pm on Saturday to 6 am on a Monday. Almost all the remaining cheap fare concessions were removed, with only a few noted examples like ship-wrecked mariners, poor children/orphans and volunteer nurses left un-touched. Season ticket holders were also faced with some severe increases and restrictions,

particularly when it was found that there was growing abuse of the system. One such abuse was from continental refugees who had set up thriving businesses in London. Fearful of the bombing raids on the city, they took to purchasing season tickets for stations on the Brighton and Thames Valley lines in order to escape for the night when an attack was on. One working to Maidenhead was so badly abused by these 'season ticket holders', railwaymen dubbed it the "Palestine Express".

By the spring of 1918 these cuts had finally appeared to have succeeded in reducing public rail travel, but when Easter came round again, the demand for tickets exceeded that for 1913 by 22%. More cuts followed, but this only saw an overall reduction of around 7% in non-military/munitions related passenger miles, indicating the British public's insatiable and un-ending desire for rail travel, despite all the means initiated to prevent if from so doing!

However, this extra coaling work presented an awkward situation, as there were insufficient men to handle all the extra work this entailed due to the enlistment of large numbers of railway staff in the forces. To meet this short-fall in staff, troops under training or prisoners of war were often drafted in to work on the railway, as can be seen at Newton Heath where coaling is being undertaken.
NATIONAL RAILWAY MUSEUM

Naval Traffic

It has been seen how well the military had prepared for the coming conflict, and all the advanced planning evolved through the Army Railway Council. Regretfully, it was not the same situation with the Admiralty, who's transport arrangements were found to be quite inadequate in the summer of 1914. It was not that the Navy did not have the required facilities, they did; however, they were mostly in the wrong places. For centuries, naval development had been geared to dealing with threats from our 'natural enemies', France and Spain, and therefore the bulk of the Admiralty's dockyards, ports and stores were situated on the southern coast between Chatham in the east, and Dartmouth in the west. As these establishments were not ideally located to deal with the new threat from across the North Sea, facilities had to be provided on the north east coasts of England and Scotland, a situation met by moving the Grand Fleet to an anchorage at Scapa Flow, between Scotland and the Orkneys, from where it would be more able to deal with the German Navy.

Those familiar with the geography of this remote region, will immediately realise what problems this presented for transporting men and essential supplies. Prior to 1914, supplies for naval craft away from the main dockyards was done by Fleet Auxiliary ships. However, supplying the Scottish anchorages by sea was inviting the attention of enemy submarines and commerce raiders, so most of this traffic was sent by rail to stations at Aberdeen, Grangemouth, Invergordon and Thurso. Traffic concerned with the fleet can roughly be divided into four groups 1) naval personnel, 2) supplies of coal and fuel oil, 3) ordnance, and 4) victuals and provisions. So complex was the movement of traffic between the main naval establishments and operational bases, it is only possible to present a brief summary in this book.

At the outbreak of the war the Navy had no facilities for sending coal by rail, yet by the end of 1919 it had secured the use of over 16,000 wagons. The bulk of these were used to carry steam coal from South Wales. Three railways, the GWR, the Rhymney, and the Taff Vale, gathered the traffic and took it to Pontypool Road (GWR), where it was marshalled into trains and forwarded to the LNWR at Warrington. At Carlisle it passed on to the Caledonian who conveyed it to Perth; there a Rail Transport Officer allocated it to the various bases to which it was forwarded by the Caledonian, Highland and Great North of Scotland railways. In later years, additional routes were used, involving the L&YR, NBR, NER and Midland companies to increase the carrying capacity. By May 1919, it was recorded that almost 5 1/2 million tons of coal had passed north of Pontypool Road, and this figure does not include that sent to English ports.

Supplies for Navy vessels were always

The Jellicoe Specials, so named after the Admiral of the Grand Fleet, can be divided into two types; those which carried coal for the fleet, and the special Euston-Thurso express trains which ran to convey officers and rating to their ships at the new naval bases in the far north. Inverness became almost a closed station, and there were numerous alterations to the station layout, with several timber-built platform extensions being erected. In the spring of 1918 a 'Jellicoe Express' arrives at the town, made up from a variety of mixed stock supplied by different companies. Of interest are the special ticket or pass barriers erected from sheep hurdles.
ROYAL NAVAL MUSEUM, PORTSMOUTH

wanted on a priority, with arrival times having to coincide with the all too short a period when a ship might be in port. Therefore goods traffic consigned for naval establishments was often sent by passenger train to ensure its arrival within the specified period. Even bulky items like propellors were sent thus, located on special wagons suitably marshalled in the passenger train. In the south traffic might be moved more leisurely to the main Naval dockyards, but in the far north there was no warehousing available for storage. A few existing warehouses were taken over to alleviate this problem, but even so, it became the norm to run special trains to provision individual ships and squadrons directly. In Scotland, this involved a whole variety of special arrangements, including the provision of many extra sidings and passing loops. At Inverness a new branch line was required to link the station with quay, it was laid and open within two weeks, despite having to demolish several houses to provide the needed access. In other places whole lines were swallowed up, as was the case with the Highland Railway's branches to Keith and Buckie, both of which were taken up to provide track for the U.S. Navy mine depot at Dalmore near Invergordon.

Following on from the adoption of the Scottish anchorages, it remained for the

Navy to arrange transport for men serving on the ships stationed there. The movement of naval personnel was, by the nature of ship movements described above, very irregular. As it was not possible to provide all the men joining or leaving their ships with accommodation on scheduled passenger trains, a naval special was run each weekday from Euston at 6 pm as from February 15th 1915, timed to arrive in Thurso at 3.30 pm the next day and involving a journey of 717 miles. At Crewe the train was joined by through coaches from Plymouth, the passengers on which would have an 834 mile journey. Connecting services were run from Milford Haven, Cardiff, Birkenhead, Liverpool, Southampton, Portsmouth, Brighton, Chatham, Dover, Tilbury, Harwich, Hull, Newcastle, Stranraer, and Barrow-in-Furness. This naval passenger system might have placed an additional burden on Britain's railways, but by it there was a regular movement between the major naval ports in England, Scotland and Wales, a system whereby naval officers and ratings, and even essential stores or supplies could be despatched to any ship or shore establishment on the mainland within 24 hours.

Tank Traffic

By the autumn of 1914, the battle-lines in France were drawn up for a war of attrition. The open battle-fields of previous centuries were replaced, and in their stead there sprang up rows of trenches. This new type of war presented a terrifying face, where countless lives were offered in a ritual sacrifice as infantry and cavalry attacks were no answer to the supremacy of machine guns. From one offensive to the next, the war continued thus for over two years. On July 1st 1916 the Battle of the Somme began, but the stalemate remained. On that first day over 60,000 British casualties were recorded, but by September neither side had made any appreciable gain and the offensive appeared to have lost its impetus. Then around 6 am on the morning of the 15th, the strongly entrenched Germans beheld block-like shapes moving ponderously out of the mists towards them. Thus began the Battle of Flers-Courcelette, where tank warfare was first employed.

Tanks had been developed by the Landships Committee, envisaged as a means for making substantial in-roads into enemy territory; using armour-plated, tracked vehicles for penetrating the forests of barbed wire and crossing vast seas of mud, impervious to withering machine-gun fire. Most British tanks came from the Metropolitan Carriage Wagon & Finance Co's works in Birmingham, but others were built by Armstrong Whitworth in Newcastle, Brown Brothers in Edinburgh, Coventry

Trainload of tanks leaving Lincoln (the Cathedral is just visible in the background of the original print), probably Mark I tanks in the very first months of tank warfare. Note that all the vehicles are sheeted over in an attempt to disguise the tanks, the rail vehicles on which they are mounted are standard types and not specially designed for the considerable weights they were asked to carry. THE TANK MUSEUM

Ordnance Works in Glasgow, Fosters of Lincoln, Kitson & Co. in Leeds, and The North British Loco Co. in Glasgow. Each of these factories had a testing ground, and when a tank had been accepted for service it would be consigned to Avonmouth Docks or the training camp at Bovington in Dorset. As these destinations were all a considerable distance from the manufacturing plants, the slow moving tanks could not cover the distance under their own power. As there were no suitable road-transporters, the railway system was the only way of moving them, though so secret was this traffic, every tank was securely sheeted down.

The earliest tanks (Mark I and two small batches of training tanks) were well outside the loading gauge, and therefore had to have their sponsons bodily removed before they could be shipped by rail. The first tank

Mark IV (female) tank, 'Auld Reekie II' of A Battalion Tank Corps. Weight 28 tons plus trench crossing fascine, bending a bolster wagon at Plateau railhead France, November 1917, before Cambrai. The transportation of tanks continued to present a problem throughout the war years for even after the development of the Rectank wagons there were never sufficient numbers of these special vehicles to entirely eliminate the use of standard rail wagons. THE TANK MUSEUM

A Mark I tank, with sponsons removed to conform with the loading gauge, mounting a wagon in the works of William Foster & Co., Lincoln. The Russian inscription reading 'With Care to Petrograd' was a naive camouflage; notice the rear steering tail that characterised the early tanks. THE TANK MUSEUM

training ground was established at Thetford, Norfolk, on the estate of Lord Iveagh. To facilitate the secret movements, the GER laid a siding into the grounds and constructed a special dock-platform so that un-loading could be accomplished out of public view. As the traffic grew, the railway company provided a further siding for one of its withdrawn dining-car sets which was sent to cater for the staff there. Once the tanks had

undergone trials, they were loaded on special trains at Barnham and despatched to either Southampton or Avonmouth. By 1918, a central testing station was opened at Newbury and when the 'secret' port of Richborough opened, all tank traffic was sent that way.

As there were no special rail-transporters, at first all tanks were carried on standard rail wagons. Mostly these were of the bogie-bolster type, despite the fact that few were really happy with the 28 ton loads placed upon them. The NER and Caledonian had a few special vehicles associated with the steel and shipbuilding industries, which were more readily suited to tank-transport. However, these were too few in number and already had enough existing commitments

as not to make any appreciable difference. Elsewhere boiler wagons were tried with some effect, but again the designs were not sufficiently suitable to produce them in the required numbers. To overcome the problem, the Railway Executive ascertained the requirements of the military and commissioned the design and manufacture of special vehicles: a transporter code-named 'RECTANK' and an associated ramp-wagon, types of which the first entered service in 1917.

At least two accidents befell tank trains, the first of which was between Sway and Brockenhurst in the New Forest. A Birmingham-Wool (for Bovington) train was crossing an embankment when a tank broke loose and swung round on its wagon. This

Plateau railhead; tank trains forming up for distribution of tanks to Battalion railheads: Battle of Cambrai, November 1917. Motive power is provided by a variety of ROD locomotives but the Army's preference for six-coupled tender engines is clearly evident.
THE TANK MUSEUM

was then hit by a north-bound train, and along with four other wagons and their loads it plunged down the embankment. The second incident occurred at Bournemouth Central, when the driver of another Bovington-bound train misjudged his braking and over-ran the signals, colliding into the rear of a stationary train.

Tanks for Bovington were detrained at Wool and driven two miles along a road to the camp. Towards the end of the war, this very substantial traffic was creating problems which were referred to the Railway

Executive. In the summer of 1918, a plan for an extension was approved with the L&SWR to supply the required track. The work was completed just after the armistice, and an 0-6-0 from the Weymouth Tramway was

allocated to provide motive power. Today, part of the camp forms the home for the historic collection of preserved armoured fighting vehicles which make up the Tank Museum.

As tank warfare developed, so did the tanks and the rail vehicles used to move them. In this view a Mark V tank is seen on a Rectank at Metropolitan Works, Birmingham. The Rectank wagons and the associated ramp wagons were specially designed by a sub-committee of the Railway Executive which was supplemented by two army officers who had assisted on the landships committee.
THE TANK MUSEUM

Air Raids

For the man in the street, Britain was an Island Fortress, the great power of the Navy providing an immense defensive wall, against everything but hit and run attacks from the German Navy. The threat from bombing seemed even more remote, for the range and capability of German aircraft was such that they would barely be able to penetrate the south eastern counties. Yet, as early as 1912, informed observers had warned of the potential threat from the great airships of Count Ferdinand von Zeppelin. However, it was an aeroplane that made the first aerial attack every experienced on Britain's railways, on Christmas Day 1914, when the LT&SR line was bombed between Standford-le-Hope and Low Street stations. The first of the airship raids was made on January 19th 1915, when Kapitan-Leutnant Fritze in Zeppelin L3 attacked Norfolk and succeeded in creating considerable damage to the railways at Kings Lynn docks. To discuss all the raids of the following four years would not be prudent, for the vast majority were almost total failures; and the damage sustained was so light, repairs were normally effected within a few hours. So we will confine our attention to more serious raids, like that at Wallsend on April 14th, when a train just avoided derailment when the track was bombed in front of it.

The east coast was frequently attacked that spring, even though the objective was the total destruction of London by a Great Fire Raid. One raid on August 12th again progressed only to the coast, but bombs dumped on Parkeston Station badly injured a loco cleaner and a fireman. On September 7th London was badly mauled, and 23 bombs fell around Euston, Holborn and Liverpool St. stations. In October a raid against the L&SWR's important junction at Croydon was less successful, though the bombs killed

The results of the air-raid on September 23rd-24th at Streatham common, where the LB&SCR signal box was badly damaged. Fortunately the box was only in use when shunting was in progress, and at the time it was un-occupied. Nevertheless, the destruction of the box caused severe inconvenience until a temporary ground-frame was installed on the 26th.

NATIONAL RAILWAY MUSEUM

nine civilians living nearby. Another Zeppelin caused damage to Leeman Street Station, which had the misfortune to be quite badly damaged two nights later in a further raid. That was the last serious raid of the year, but on January 31st 1916 the attacks were resumed with a vengeance. In an extensive raid on the Midlands, severe damage was caused to railway installations at Wednesbury, Tipton and Burton. In Derby, the raiders specifically aimed their attention at the Midland Railway's headquarters, doing their best to destroy the works. Large sections of the plant were damaged, causing severe disruption to all departments. A similar raid was planned against Sheffield on March 5th, but prevailing head winds forced the airships to dump their bombs on Humberside. Damage was done to the GCR's electric tramway and steam lines at Immingham Halt, but it was just one of the 53 Zeppelin raids this district suffered.

On March 31st, attention was turned

against the munition factories, particularly those at Stowmarket, Erith and Woolwich Arsenal. But once again the raiders had little success. Three weeks later, a bomb was dropped at Fairlop on the Chigwell line, wrecking the station master's house. The raids of September 2nd-3rd became known as 'Zepp Sunday' when no less than eighteen enemy airships left their bases to attack England. Despite the size of the attacking force little damage is recorded to railway property; the only serious problem was at Boston, where a GNR signalman was badly injured. That night the first Zeppelin was shot down, and this signalled the end of the great raids. Though in a sneak attack on September 23rd, the stations at Streatham Common and Streatham Hill were struck by 600lb bombs. More bombs were dropped at Nottingham, causing damage to both the GNR and GCR lines out of the city.

On June 13th 1917, three bombs landed on Liverpool Street Station during a daylight

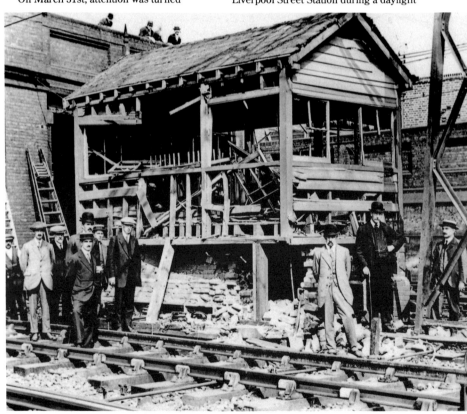

In ARP development, the railways played an important role, with several anti-aircraft weapons being designed and produced in railway workshops. This was not all, for at least two workshops were involved in the production of shells and tracer bullets designed to bring down the giant German airships. To illuminate the raiders as they passed over the cities, giant search-lights were produced in large numbers, a small batch of which were converted from naval types at the GNR's Doncaster plant.
NATIONAL RAILWAY MUSEUM

raid. The 12 noon train for Hunstanton standing at Platform 8 was badly damaged, and two coaches standing in the adjacent bay platform received a direct hit. These were in use as a medical centre for the recruiting service; as a result, sixteen men were killed and 23 injured. An equally nasty raid came on the night of September 29th/30th when a projectile crashed through the roof of the drivers' dormitory at Stratford, killing one driver outright and injuring two others. Three locomotives nearby were slightly damaged. On January 28th 1918, a train of empty carriages was hit as it left Cannon Street Station, considerably damaging one third class coach. But probably the worst attack of all was on March 17th, when five bombs fell in the vicinity of St. Pancras Station and the Midland Grand Hotel. One failed to explode, but the other four claimed 20 lives, mostly people sheltering under a covered carriage drive leading from the hotel to the main booking hall. The last of the German raids was August 5th 1918, when three airships approached Great Yarmouth. One was shot down and the two remaining craft turned and fled for home. In all, 24 railway workers were killed during bombing between December 1914 and August 1918.

The Humber ports of Grimsby, Hull and Immingham, and to a lesser extent Goole, were the frequent targets of German Zeppelins. Often Hull was as far as they could reach because of strong head-winds, and they would dump their bombs willy-nilly across any likely target they saw. However, and unlike the raids of World War 2, the attacks resulted in minimal damage. The strength of the explosives was very light, as can be seen by the crater left by a bomb which landed in between a series of timber sidings served by the Hull & Barnsley Railway.
CITY OF KINGSTON UPON HULL, MUSEUMS & ART GALLERIES

Accidents & disasters

As might be appreciated, the level of rail traffic grew considerably during World War One, a considerable proportion of which involved the transportation of highly dangerous consignments, including explosives and poisonous gasses. In addition, railway safety was prejudiced by a number of dangerous factors, including 1) increased troop and naval traffic, 2) transfer of coast-wise traffic from shipping to railways, 3) the enlistment of railwaymen in the armed forces and their replacement by less experienced staff, 4) the Ministry of Munitions' refusal to release much needed material for the maintenance of locos and stock, and 5) significantly lower standards of track maintenance and replacement. Those who have read our companion series, Trains In Trouble, will recognise all this as presenting the recipe for disaster. As many of the accidents between August 1914 and December 1918 have been discussed in that series, it is not intended to cover the same ground in these pages.

The year 1915 might be considered as the most horrific, for it was to see four exceptionally bad accidents. The scene was set on New Year's Day, when the driver of a Great Eastern express from Clacton to

Quintinshill was undoubtedly one of the most horrific accidents ever recorded in British railway history. The facts concerning the accident have been well documented in the Trains In Trouble series, but the role the war played in the events that fateful May morning are not so widely known. Firstly, all the trains involved were military specials or busier than normal because of the war. Added to this, the passing loops all down the Caley line were in continuous use due to the excessive number of additional trains using the route. Indeed, those loops were so continuously used, it is a wonder that the sloppy working practices at Quintinshill had not led to an accident before. Finally, despite the fact that a large number of men were gathered in the box when signalman Tinsley cleared his signals for the troop train, they were all too preoccupied discussing newspaper war reports to notice his mistake.

Upper picture: The twisted and mangled wreckage that was once a train.

Lower picture: The pitiful number of survivors from the troop train stand in a field alongside the line whilst an officer reads out the roll-call.

BOTH DUMFRIES & GALLOWAY LIBRARY SERVICE – DUMFRIES REFERENCE LIBRARY

London failed to stop at a distant signal. At the west end of Ilford station it struck a local train to Gidea Park in a violent side-long collision which claimed 10 lives and resulted in 500 injuries. On Easter Monday there was a spectacular run-away and crash at Burnham, on the Somerset & Dorset Joint. Yet this was nothing on the scale of what was to follow on May 15th, when a five-train crash occurred at a way-side passing loop north of Gretna. In the carnage at Quintinshill, over 227 lives were lost, with 224 more injured, a figure which has never been exceeded in any British railway disaster. On August 14th the spectre of inadequate maintenance reared its ugly head at Weedon, when the Irish Mail was derailed at high-speed. The simple loss of a pin and locking collar claiming no less than ten dead and 64 injured. In almost ghoulish glee, the mis-fortune which had dogged 1915 decided to have a final fling just two weeks before the end of the year at St. Bede's Junction on the North Eastern Railway. There a signalman's error, and a lack of diligence by the driver of a banking engine lead to a double collision which was attended by a fire; the disaster accounted for 18 lives and left 81 passengers with injuries and burns.

The year 1916 kicked off with something even more spectacular, though fortunately not very serious, when the Penistone Viaduct collapsed. On the viaduct at the time was an L&YR tank engine, which was precipitated to the bottom of the Don Valley. An urgent shortage of locomotives saw some remarkable attempts to recover the engine, but the steep sided valley and the atrocious weather prevented a successful outcome. After the comparative quiet of 1916, a major accident at Ratho on the North British Railway claimed twelve lives on January 3rd 1917. On September 15th a rake of ten six-wheeled NER coaches forming a troop train

When Penistone viaduct collapsed tank engine No. 661 was thrown to the bed of the valley. Despite the sheer drop, it was not badly damaged. In view of the very acute traffic situation a concerted effort was made to recover it from it lay. Regretfully all the attempts failed due to the steepness of the valley sides, and the atrocious weather conditions that February. Eventually the unfortunate engine was cut up on site and the remains were hauled away to Horwich works in wagons.
AUTHOR'S COLLECTION

ran away down the branch railway at Catterick Camp, derailing on a sharp curve and killing three soldiers. A fortnight later another NER engine came to grief near Hawes Junction, when the locomotive's leading axle snapped. January 1918 saw another bad start to the year, as seven fatalities are recorded at Little Salkeld, where a Midland Railway locomotive was derailed by a landslide. This list is by no means comprehensive, but it is representative of such accidents as befell the railways during the war.

Of the other accidents and disasters much could be written, but perhaps the last few words should be said about those relating to explosives traffic. In the autumn of 1916, two accidents involving munitions trains on the Caledonian railway were remarkably free from any serious consequences. Then, on September 22nd 1917, a train of cordite and ammunition being conveyed by the LB&SCR was threatened when one of the vans caught fire. A goods inspector, C. J. Carne, bravely un-coupled the van, and with other members of staff succeeded in extinguishing the flames. For his gallantry, Mr. Carne was awarded the Albert Medal by King George V

on December 18th. Regretfully the same diligence was not exercised by his colleagues on April 18th 1918, when another LB&SCR munitions train broke in two inside Redhill Tunnel. The guard took no action for over ten minutes, and was thereby unable to prevent another freight engine, No. 541, running into the obstruction. Under the impression that nothing was amiss, the signalman allowed a train carrying naval artillery shells into the tunnel in the opposite direction. All three trains were compressed inside the bore, and despite 26 wagons being completely broken up, incredibly no fire started and none of the explosives were detonated. However, the most serious incident must be that near Bradford in the summer of 1916. A fire at the Low Moor Chemical Company was followed by an explosion, the results of which devastated Low Moor. The railway sidings were hit by a fire-ball, and the nearby gas works also exploded: at least 34 were left dead, but even today the true facts have never been made public.

By contrast with Penistone the explosion alongside the L&YR line at Low Moor on August 22nd 1916, was one of the worst civilian disasters of the war. Quite what started the fire at the chemical works south of the junction may never be known, but it has been claimed that a metal drum containing picric acid crystals was being rolled along the ground at the time.

The upper view shows the aftermath at Low Moor Junction with the branch to Heckmondwike curving away from the main Halifax-Bradford line. Over 100 wrecked wagons and vans, 30 burnt-out coaches, dozens of roof-less houses and the remains of the gas-holder all testify to the force of the explosion. Most people living nearby took shelter in the tunnel, but one lady remained in her house to tend to the stone of bread she had just put in the oven – remarkably she emerged unscathed.

The lower view is of No. 1 Signal Box after the explosion with smashed windows and broken slates being the only serious damage despite the fire-storm which swept across the adjacent tracks, consuming almost everything in its way. It is reported that at least 34 people were killed, and railway company first-aid staff were called in to render assistance. In all some 45 members of the L&YR staff received awards for gallantry because of their actions that day.

NATIONAL RAILWAY MUSEUM

Locomotives for abroad

The study of locomotive use during the period 1914-18 is a long and complex subject and though we hope to discuss it fully in a later volume, for the present we can roughly divide it into three separate areas: 1) locomotives for home use by the individual railway companies; 2) locomotives specially built for military service; and 3) locomotives requisitioned by the Government for use at home and overseas. Of these groups, we are concerned with the latter; for it presents the most interesting facets of civilian railways at war, in addition to having a direct bearing on the reduction of rail services in this country.

Railway companies had been asked by Army Railway Council as early as 1905, to provide a supply of locomotives if war should break out overseas. This request had been repeated in 1911, but in considering all the needs of the Army Railway Council (and its successor the War Railway Council), it appears as though this was the most difficult request for the railway companies to grant. It seems as though they were willing to assist, but only if a substantial compensation were paid. An alternative to this 'replacement value' compensation was proffered by J. A. F. Aspinall and H. A. Walker in 1912, whereby the companies would make available non-standard or surplus locomotives for Government service at 'book value'. The council refused to accept this

offer, seeing it only as an excuse for the companies to dump their rubbish on the War Office. Thereafter the matter lay, with little progress being made on either side.

Consequently, on the declaration of war the Army found itself without the required number of locomotives, for even the shortest of campaigns. The situation was not helped by the quick German advance on Paris, which though repulsed, saw the invaders wrecking whole sections of the French railway system as they retreated. It was therefore quite clear that not only were locomotives and drivers required, but a whole railway system would have to be created to supply the army's needs in France. It was also evident by the end of 1914 that both operating and construction corps would have to be formed, but during that first winter the whole question became as bogged down as transport in the

The two largest batches of locomotives sent to the ROD in France were those 8-coupled locomotives of the GCR and NER. The NER 0-8-0 locos were the Class T (LNER Q5), of which NER No. 660/ROD No. 5660 built at Darlington in June 1907 is an example. Some 50 of these engines were allocated to the ROD, and were largely employed on the heavy stone trains from the Marquise Quarries near Boulogne. The engines were returned to their owner during the first six months of 1919, with the majority being shipped on the Richborough Train Ferry.
NATIONAL RAILWAY MUSEUM

quagmire of the Western Front. The situation was far more formidable than at first envisaged, and it was not until April 1915 that the Railway Executive undertook the formation of Railway Operating Division, Royal Engineers, on behalf of the War Office.

The ROD was created by drafting a few officers from the Railway Transport Establishment, but the greatest proportion of men were recruited from the railway companies themselves. At first the division consisted of a mechanical section and an operating section, each comprised of three officers and 260 NCOs and sappers. Cecil Paget, General Superintendent of the Midland Railway was appointed Officer Commanding, later attaining the rank of Lt.-Colonel. The men were trained at Longmoor, and then sent to France where they initially took over the Belgian locomotives brought there after the fall of Belgium. The numbers grew steadily, and in July a third section was sent overseas, comprised of men drawn entirely from the LNWR. By the end of 1918 the number of British railwayman attached to the ROD was in excess of 24,000. In addition to this, eight companies of civilian platelayers numbering around 2,000 men were sent out to France from March 1917 onwards; included in the number were about 300 men who were over 60 years of age. All this indicates the substantial railway development initiated to feed the front line, carrying in replacement troops, ammunition and supplies, bringing out the maimed and wounded. The French

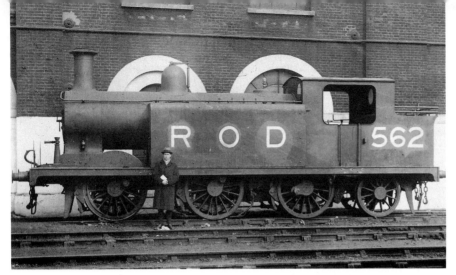

In preparation for service with the ROD, a LBSCR Class E4 No. 562 is seen at Brighton works in November 1917. Formerly called *Laughton*, the 0-6-2T was allocated to Tunbridge Wells shed. After being shipped to France via Dover and Calais, it was put to work on the Audruicq Ammunition Depot, along with other members of the class. They were later moved nearer to the front, but were forced to retreat when the Germans advanced on Arras. Thereafter they worked around Doullens, but after the armistice until the summer of 1919, they performed sterling duties on the Doullens-Arras direct line.
NATIONAL RAILWAY MUSEUM

network was just about shattered, especially the Nord system, of which only about 45% of the pre-war mileage remained in Allied control. Generally, it appears as though what sections of the French railways that were still running, were largely dependent on the efforts of British railwaymen. By the autumn of 1916, 490 French main-line locomotives and 54 shunting engines were in the employ of the British army, but even this was not enough. Director General of Transportation, Sir Eric Geddes, advised the War Office that to meet coming demands, at least 156 British locomotives would be needed in France. The French said the true figure was likely to be nearer 900. At the time there were 54 British locomotives working in France, and after further consultation it was reported that 2-300 locomotives and 10-20,000 wagons would be needed to support the planned British offensives the following spring. The railways were at a loss to see how this could be accomplished, even with substantial cuts in passenger services. By December 1916 the demand for main-line locomotives had

increased to 370 and the Railway Executive despatched a sub-committee to France to investigate the situation. In February it became evident that even this high number had substantially increased, when it was revealed that the British authorities in France had undertaken to provide 709 locomotives. Of these 368 had been ordered or provided, but this still left the depleted British companies with the task of finding a further 341. In addition, the War Office indicated that 81 locomotives were required for the coming Egyptian campaign. During the summer of 1917 the Locomotive Engineers sub-committee took a hard look at

the situation, which revealed that 420 engines had already been despatched to France. However, when they looked at the motive power situation at home, they discovered that a very considerable number of locomotives were stopped awaiting repair due to the lack of men and materials required to rectify them. It was evident, with 1,400 engines over and above the normal number out of service, that a serious disruption of home services would ensue that autumn. All of this posed the executive with an horrendous situation, without even considering how a further 600 engines could be released. It was a matter which could only be addressed by carrying out a physical assessment of what locomotives the companies had, and what they actually required to meet their commitments. Under a system of pooling and combined allocation,

A group of L&YR engines assembled for despatch to France are gathered round a coal stage. About one third of the total number of the L&YR locomotives supplied to the ROD are pictured here. All were Aspinall 0-6-0 tender goods engines, and were consecutively numbered from 1700 to 1731. All were built between 1889 and 1895, but despite their age, they performed valuable service in France and were greatly admired by the drivers who operated with them.

NATIONAL RAILWAY MUSEUM

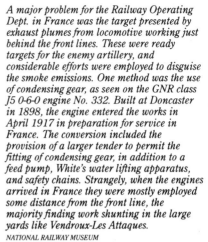

the companies were able to release 123 locomotives to France, and a further 32 to the middle-East. At home the pooling resulted in considerable numbers of locomotives being loaned to other companies, with some strange workings being recorded as a result.

The following table records the total allocation of locomotives and stock loaned or sold to the Government by the British railway companies up to December 1918. The figures in parenthesis indicates where the numbers returned differs from those loaned.

Company	Locos	Wagons	Coaches
Caledonian	25	–	25
Furness	–	–	6
G&SWR	–	–	7
Great Central	33	3,267 (3,204)	20(18)
Great Eastern	43	–	–
G.N. of Scotland	–	–	31
Great Northern	26	1,000(933)	–
Great Western	73(57)	5,772(5,694)	27
Hull & Barnsley	–	–	20
L&YR	32	1,560(1,487)	–
LBSCR	12		2
LNWR	111(64)	6,370(6,119)	90(89)
LSWR	–	–	94(93)
Midland	78	6,128(6,008)	6(677)
Midland & GN Joint	–	20(19)	20
North British	25	–	–
North Eastern	50	4,545(4,448)	–
North Staffs	–	–	16
S&ECR	8	1,042(1,031)	24(23)

Concurrent with this demand for main-line and shunting locomotives, there was an additional requirement for narrow-gauge equipment to link the front lines with the supply depots in the rear. This development expanded greatly from the winter of 1916 onwards, by which time most of the roads in France and Belgium had been shelled out of existence, and as a result the supply lines were little more than a quagmire of mud and shell craters. The use of horses, motor vehicles and conventional steam locomotives was totally impractical, so to address the problem the Royal Engineers set about laying down a series of 2ft gauge lines from supply depots to the 'front'. As steam locomotives were often too heavy even in this gauge, and because exhaust steam made an excellent target for enemy artillery spotters, it was decided to employ light-weight locomotives with internal combustion engines. Accordingly a number of armour-plated 0-4-0s were purchased from a firm called Motor Rail and shipped to France in 1917 where they performed a sterling service. After the armistice many of these machines were repatriated to Britain and sold into industrial service, a use for which they were eminently suited.

Prisoners of War and Refugees

During the four and a half years of the war, and a considerable time thereafter, there was a significant traffic in those who might be termed 'the unfortunates of war': those individuals who had been ousted not only from their homes, but also their homelands. Refugees flocked to Britain throughout the war years, but of these the most numerous were Belgian. The majority arrived without any possessions, and were thus largely dependant on charity. Such aid was freely given, though it was expected that the refugees should find employment in one of the Munition works, whilst men of military age would join one of the Belgian army brigades. For both these groups, the Railway Executive was directed by the Government to provide free rail travel. In respect of Belgian railwaymen, who might be of use either here or in France, the Executive appointed a sub-committee under Mr. A. Watson of the L&YR. He placed four rooms in his Westminster offices at the disposal of the committee, and here a small staff of railwaymen were able to direct their colleagues from Belgium into occupations suited to their training. Other sub-committees handled free travel for the refugees, and for Belgian soldiers on leave from France.

Records concerning the actual movement of prisoners of war are very scarce, and of those I consulted, none revealed any new information. However, this substantial traffic continued throughout the war years, and can be sub-divided into three categories: 1) the movement of German POWs during the war, and their eventual repatriation, 2) the recovery of British POWs after the armistice, and 3) the repatriation of any prisoner during the war years, when he was obviously ill or unfit for further military service (a little known, but widespread work carried on under the auspices of the Geneva Red Cross Commission). It is only possible to guess at the extent of POW traffic, but it emerges that the majority of German POWs were landed at Avonmouth, Southampton, Liverpool and Cardiff, and then transferred to the camps. Of those Germans who were repatriated before December 1918, it seems that the ports of Leith and Newcastle were used, as such transfers were through the

Belgian railway workes, many of them from skilled grades (ie drivers, signalmen, station masters, etc) were directed on to menial jobs on Britain's railways to replace Railwaymen who had enlisted. This often meant they were used as labourers, plate-layers, and as in this case – goods porters. In the middle of 1915 three Belgian railwaymen are seen along with the NER counterparts unloading bananas at Annfield Plain Station.
NORTH OF ENGLAND OPEN AIR MUSEUM, BEAMISH

offices of the Red Cross in Sweden. A counter-balancing arrangement was in operation for the exchange of sick British prisoners, though it seems that on their return these men were landed at Leith, Hartlepool and Hull. After the armistice, the repatriation traffic was a veritable flood and a variety of rail and ferry routes were used to convey the two-way traffic.

The following example may serve as an indication of the vast prisoner of war traffic: In 1915 a group of German prisoners were loaded into a train at Southampton. The doors of the 6-wheeled coaches had been nailed shut down one side, with half the doors on the other side similarly treated. Arriving in Wales, the captives were

marched to a camp and sorted into categories. One group of soldiers were mixed with a number of naval ratings, and they found that they all had an engineering back-ground. The group of around 50 were then sent to a camp near Carno, where they stayed for some weeks. Eventually a British major arrived, and told them that they were to be given a chance of making amends for the damage their Kaiser had done. Mystified, the men were loaded onto a train and taken on a long journey into the North of England. On arrival, they found themselves in Weardale, Co. Durham. Here they were marched over miles of barren moorland to reach an isolated village. For three and a half years the men remained here, working on a mine and quarry railway system. Most were involved in construction work, but many progressed to responsible jobs like incline brakemen, and in one case an engine driver. After the war, some decided to settle among the community who had accepted them as men, and not just the enemy, and I am indebted to one of them for recounting this story.

In the category of prisoners, we might look at another group: prisoners, not of war but of conscience. It is not widely recognized, but there were large numbers of men who refused to take up military service. A few may have been cowards, but the vast majority were men of principle and mostly belonged to religious or political organisations which refused to take sides in the issue. Prominent among these groups were the Quakers and the Jehovah's Witnesses, and despite the intense pressure put upon them to fight, most ended up in penal servitude here in Britain. Many were sent to the high security jail at Princetown, and were set to work on cultivating the harsh barren wastes of Dartmoor. By 1916, so many conscientious objectors were being sent to Dartmoor, Portland and other West Country prisons that the GWR began running special trains, the prisoners being chained for most of the journey. Interestingly, in another journey the GWR conveyed an important train with a cargo consigned to Bodmin Jail: in this instance the load was none other than the Crown Jewels which were being removed from the Tower of London for safe keeping.

Women at War

Those readers who have studied the corresponding chapter in volume one of this series, will recognise the vital and demanding roles undertaken by women during World War II. One might therefore expect a similar comparison with female railway labour between 1914 and 1918, especially when it is revealed that the peak number of women thus employed reached 68,801 in September 1918. Though there is no doubt that female labour was of immense value during this period, it must be realised that extreme prejudice was manifested in certain quarters. At the outbreak of war, the value of women workers was just becoming recognised, but in some industries an 'all-male' attitude still predominated. This was especially so in the railway industry, where in 1913 only 13,046 women were employed. Of these 8,482 were in 'domestic' categories, such as cleaners, waitresses, hotel staff and washer-women. Only 4,564 were employed on railway work proper, and of these most were in the clerical grades. Only in a very few instances had women progressed to more responsible positions.

All this was changed by the number of men joining the army, or called up for duties with the 'railway troops'. The labour situation became so acute by March 1915, that the Railway Executive formed a sub-committee to look at the employment of women in grades formerly occupied by men. They found that most of the clerical work, ticket

Women working on the railway were not always allocated light duties, as this picture at the Derby coal stack testifies. Some 15 ladies are pictured whilst engaged in the arduous work on May 3rd 1917, with the male crew of the depot's 25 ton crane which is being used to lift the coal skips.
NATIONAL RAILWAY MUSEUM

collection, and carriage cleaning duties could be handled by women, as could some porterage, engineering and maintenance work. Obviously, heavy duties such as engine driving and firing could not be considered, though a proposal was made that women could also be used in the quieter branch-line signal boxes. It is understood that the first woman to fill this role was at porter/signalman at Netherton Station (L&YR). As it might be expected, women excelled in clerical grades, but they also did well in other areas, for example carriage cleaning. In this regard it was found that women only managed to accomplish two thirds of the productivity of their male counterparts, but the work was of such a high standard (both internally and externally), women cleaners endeared themselves to the travelling public.

By August 1915, the committee was faced with a dilemma, for it was evident that on average three women were required to fill the roles of two men. Additionally, the percentage of women leaving after just one month's service was an alarming 42%, with a further 21% resigning after two months. A large part of the problem was that all the jobs were temporary, a fact insisted on by the National Union of Railwaymen in the protection of its members' jobs when they had enlisted. As there was no career structure, and indeed no family tradition to follow, women in the most un-rewarding jobs soon packed them in and found employment in the munitions factories where they could earn £11 per week. In times of peace a young man, say the son of an engine driver, would start with the company at the bottom; probably cleaning the very engines that one day (with effort and dedication) he would eventually fire, then drive. Such career moves were not possible to women, and thus the dedication was largely missing.

Yet, in many ways women excelled in their new careers, and a partial list of professions, is recorded at the end of 1916 as: Clerks (13,904), carriage cleaners (2,173),

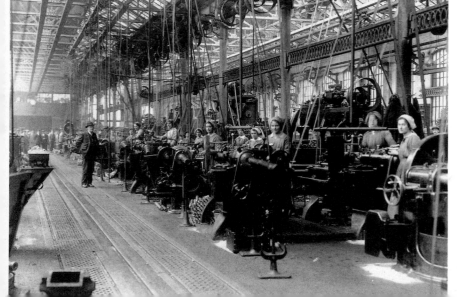

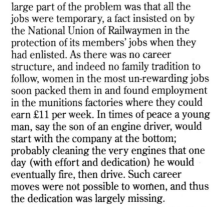

In the workshops women soon became adept at engineering tasks which were part of 'continuous runs', though they were less able at 'one-off' jobs. During 1917, male and female workers pose for an official photograph in the Machine Shop at Horwich Works.
NATIONAL RAILWAY MUSEUM

workshop women (1,278), platform porters (1,098), munition workers (1,046), goods porters (901), ticket collectors (706), gate-keepers (705), engine cleaners (587), labourers (239), machinists (178), messengers (150), parcel porters (147), sack-repairers (121), painters (99), dining-car attendants (93), number-takers (79), page-girls (40), weighing-machine attendants (23), brass lacquerers (23), letter-sorters (15), signal'men' (14), horse-keepers (14), carters (12), train attendants (11), cloak-room attendants (10), luggage-room porters (10), wagon-repairers (8), hotel porters (6), harness-cleaners (6), warehouse-women (5), crockery-collectors (4), information attendants (4), ferry attendants (2), bridge-keepers (2), blind-pullers (2), flag-makers (2). There was also one woman found in each of the following occupations, gardeners, carver, printer, billiard-maker, signal cleaner/lighter, lamp room attendant, concrete-maker, canal attendant, halt-attendant, crane driver, lock-keeper, coil-maker, time-keeper, and call girl (though one suspects this was a more innocent occupation than the name might imply today!).

Another interesting group of women railway workers were those enrolled into the North Eastern Railway's police force. These railway police-women are pictured at York in 1916, and their duties were almost identical to their male counterparts, and throughout the war they acquitted themselves with distinction. Additional duties ranged from guarding railway yards to assisting the military police in the apprehension of deserters and those men who over-stayed their leave.
NATIONAL RAILWAY MUSEUM

The same returns showed that many companies had made substantial use of female labour, as for instance the GCR which had employed just 70 female clerks in 1913, and was now served by 1,526 women in that grade. Other companies maintained the prejudice, for of the 130 companies controlled by the Executive, only 68 had increased their pre-war female labour force by more than 10%. Ten of them employed none. By the end of the war men filtered back to their occupations, but in 1920 over 20,000 women were still employed in grades where their talents had become appreciated, and thus the 'male only' mould was broken. The results of this pioneering work was to become evident inside two decades, when women were to assume even greater responsibilities on Britain's railways in times of war.

Munition Works & Traffic

In view of the colossal amount of munition traffic carried in the first year of the war, a Ministry of Munitions Transport Branch was established in September 1915. The branch was sub-divided in to four sections, A. B, C and D. In turn each of these were divided into eight sub-sections, and each had an area of individual responsibility; for example, C.M. 8 was the Forwarding & Delivery dept. As such it was primarily concerned with rail traffic and all technical matters pertaining thereto, and provided advice where special facilities (like new sidings) might be required. The work was so extensive, that by February 1916, C.M.8 became the Munitions Railway Transport Branch, which was then sub-divided into eight different sections. It served various branches of the Ministry, but chiefly the, Mechanical Warfare, Gun-ammunition Filling, Trench Warfare Supply, and Explosives Supply departments. To carry out this work, it had area offices at Newcastle, Manchester, Leeds, Birmingham, Cardiff, Bristol, London, and two in Glasgow. Most of these offices had several sub-offices, and these were nearly all based in, or near, railway stations. The role of these Area Offices was, basically, to inform the railway companies about the priority of shipments, to minimise waste journeys, arrange for sufficient wagons to be available, and to keep the Ministry fully informed on a weekly basis.

The Branch endeavoured to ensure more efficient use of resources, particularly tank wagons which were in exceptionally short supply. It also had considerable problems finding vans fitted with sorbo-rubber matting, such as those used for the transportation of volatile chemicals like nitro-glycerine and picric acid. It was evident that short distance trips, especially those around London, Birmingham, Lancashire and the

The number of shells which were daily discharged by allied guns must have reached astronomic figures, as might be understood when one considers the vast mountain of shell-cases pictured here is just a very small part of the empty cases returned to Britain for filling. The shells are seen at Doncaster Works (GNR), but similar stock-piles were seen at Derby, Gorton, Horwich, Stratford, Swindon and Wolverhampton. Many of the shells arrived back at the works in a split condition and had to be scraped, but in 1916 the GWR experts at Swindon discovered a way of brazing splits up to $1^1/_2$ inches long and thereafter the GER specialised in this avenue of the re-forming work.
NATIONAL RAILWAY MUSEUM

West Riding were making unreasonable demands on the vehicles available. Therefore they endeavoured to send consignments of less than fifteen miles distance by road: this produced tremendous savings. In Liverpool alone, over 23,000 tons of munitions was switched to the roads in October 1918. Only

by a very rigid check of vehicles, and central pooling, were the Munition Transport Officers able to keep the voluminous supplies moving.

It would be virtually impossible to document all the work of the Branch, and even to list the various rail-served munition works, shell-filling factories, and stores would be difficult. Establishments like Gretna, Erith, Woolwich, all deserve coverage, but space does not permit. Therefore, I have drawn on just a few specific examples, which serve to indicate the enormous level of this traffic. Naturally, some lines carried significantly more munition traffic than others, and whilst it might be expected on those routes leading to the embarkation ports, that on some other lines is quite surprising. Because of the potentially dangerous loads, munition trains tended to be restricted to certain routes. Generally, this led to trains being routed away from urban areas, and many took circuitous routes to reach their destination. In London it was a different matter, for the munition factories around the metropolis were forced to send this traffic through built-up areas night and day. For example, the munition factory at Hayes despatched an average of 8 trains per day, each contained upwards of 50 wagons and required double-heading. Most of these were routed via the West London lines, and worked as block trains by the L&SWR all the way to the ferry terminal at Richborough. So great was the volume of ammunition traffic on the West

London line, that it was necessary to keep the signal boxes almost continuously open. Even the tiniest of branches found

---

Despite the introduction of the Iron Mink standard, the number of gunpowder vans was totally inadequate for war needs between 1914-18. As will have been noted earlier, many companies converted existing vehicles into 'Special Gunpowder Vans' which were thus named in order to free them from the pending legislation concerning the movement of explosives by train. Other companies built new vans to the old designs in order to meet the immediate demand; the GNR for example produced a batch of 8-ton vans at Doncaster in August 1915, in which No. 23572 was included. The vehicles were short-lived and none were left in service by the grouping at the end of 1922.

NATIONAL RAILWAY MUSEUM

themselves carrying munitions, as exampled by the Balloch branch. This 5 mile long NBR/CR joint line from the bonny banks of Loch Lomond down to Dumbarton, conveyed countless thousands of shell casings and finished shells that were produced in the district. On some main lines, significant problems were encountered by the sheer volume of this traffic, including the section of the Caledonian Railway where it passed into England. So great was the flow of munition traffic between Gretna and Carlisle, that the company was unable to cope. This was reported back to the Railway Executive and within three weeks the Ministry of Munitions had approved, and provided £60,000 for widening the line between Floriston and Rockliffe.

Another major form of traffic governed by the Branch, was that of picric acid. This was a major constituent in most explosives, and

our pre-war needs had been largely supplied by the Essen Dye-works in Germany. When these chemicals became un-available the dye-works in Britain were unable to cope, so in 1915-6 the Government provided resources to set up new plants in the textile producing areas. One of the leading dye experts of the time, Major L. B. Holliday was released from war service to establish a picric plant and munitions works at Bradley near Huddersfield. The Ministry of Munitions were persuaded to lay in a two-mile system of sidings, connected to the LNWR line, and operated (like most other munition sites) with fire-less locos. Holliday seized the opportunity, and built a large dye-works on an adjoining site at Deighton, laying in more sidings to serve it. Alas, his unauthorised scheme was discovered and the Government refused to pay for the additional work.

The role of the Railway Workshops

From the very outset of the war in August 1914, it became evident that the necessities of the conflict would quickly out-strip the capacity for producing the required supplies. This placed the government in an awkward position, which could only be addressed by the utilisation of civilian factories for war-production. In this regard, the railway companies became directly involved in the manufacture of a variety of supplies for the armed forces. The work at first was low-key, and of such a nature as to not have too great an effect on routine business in the various locomotive works and carriage and wagon shops: constructions of special military needs, like the ambulance or armoured trains being in effect, just normal railway work.

The Railway Executive initially agreed to the use of railway workshops, on the proviso that it did not materially affect the companies' ability to fulfil its needed work of the repair and replacement of railway equipment. Happily the leading companies agreed that they could assist, and in the autumn of 1914 the workshops at Ashford, Barassie, Brighton, Cowlairs, Crewe, Darlington, Derby, Doncaster, Duckinfield, Earlstown, Eastleigh, Gateshead, Glasgow, Gorton, Horwich, Lancing, Newton Heath, St. Rollox, Stratford, Swindon, Temple Mills, Wolverton and York began work for the war effort. The first order was for the ambulance trains which we will discuss later, to be followed on September 2nd by a request for 12,250 stretchers. A fortnight later, an order was received for 5,000 general service wagons (road). This figure was then increased to 6,000, whilst the stretcher order was more than doubled by the end of the year. Orders were received for the conversion of 500, 10 ton covered goods vans to military use, with supplies to begin reaching Government depots by November. Soon the workshops were entering the field of munitions and armament manufacture, and the resulting pressure this caused was referred to the Railway Executive.

In October 1914, a Railway War Manufactures Sub-Committee was established to regulate the flow of this work, and where possible make better use of existing facilities in the different workshops. The names of the members of that committee testify to its importance, for it was comprised of such notable figures as: Henry Fowler, C. H. Dent, H. N. Gresley, George Hughes, G. J. Churchward and C. J. Bowen Cooke; if this were not enough, the group was later to include A. J. Hill, P. Drummond, W. Pickersgill, J. G. Robinson and Vincent Raven. the sub-committee had to decide three pre-requisites before agreeing to the acceptance of any war work at the railway workshops, these being: Could such work be done, a) under present conditions, b) if railway repair work were curtailed, or c) if extra plant were laid down with the government supplying such plant or the capital for its cost? Option a) was almost impossible because of the number of railway employees who had enlisted in the armed forces, though the Government agreed to release such men if they were willing to return. Many did, but even so, it was largely options b) and c) which had to be adopted.

By the end of the year, around 31 companies were actively involved in Government production or related sub-contract work, though strange to relate, this number had not substantially increased at

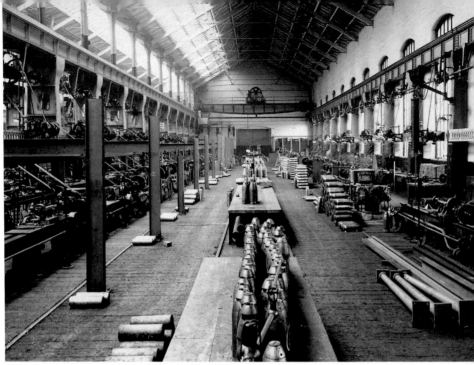

As indicated in the previous chapter, shell manufacture assumed phenomenal proportions in the railway workshops from 1915 onwards. In addition to all the re-forming work, thousands of new cases, fuses, adaptors and gaines were produced. The NER at Darlington turned out around 1¹/₂ million complete shells during the war, and even the little L&Y did considerable munitions work at Horwich. Over 142,000 fuses were made, of Mk 101, Mk 102 and Mk 103 varieties. Shells up 13.5 inch were manufactured in the works, though this view in the erecting shop shows newly produced shells of a smaller calibre.
NATIONAL RAILWAY MUSEUM

the end of the war. It is difficult to cover all the aspects of war production at the railway workshops, for the official list of the different items produced between August 1914 December 1918 amounts to no less than a 121 page document. Much of the early work was, however, still closely related to the peace-time activities of the workshops and the involvement therefore caused little hardship to companies. It became the rule that if a particular works had spare capacity, or could achieve such capacity by temporarily postponing less urgent work,

The L&YR (and a number of other railway works) did not just limit itself to the manufacture of shells, but also produced the instruments required to propel them as well. In direct liaison with the Royal Arsenal at Woolwich they produced castings for various types of heavy ordnance. Later complete guns were produced, like the 8in howitzer which stands in the erecting shop along with locomotives in various states of construction or repair. Note the track of the 18in gauge works railway on the floor of the shop.
NATIONAL RAILWAY MUSEUM

then it would accept the Government orders. Unfortunately, this position changed dramatically in 1915, when the supply of shells to the Western Front was found to be totally inadequate. Following the catastrophic attack at Lislie on May 4th 1915, the *Times* recorded that the British failure was due to a lack of high explosives to level the enemy positions – compared to the French, whom it seemed, were in the position of being able to fire 276 rounds per gun. The matter was raised in Parliament on May 14th, and the following day the Railway Executive Committee were asked if some of its workshops could be turned over for the necessary production. On June 8th 1915, Royal Assent was given for the formation of the Ministry of Munitions, and within days of its inception, orders for machining 2,250 shells a week were issued to the Executive. The principal capacity was to be provided by seven companies: the GCR, GER, GNR, GWR, LNWR, L&YR and NER, who in turn would distribute the work around their various workshops. In addition, the GWR was asked to cast some 2,000 6 inch high-explosive shells every week.

Even though the Government assisted by releasing over 2,650 skilled machinists from the armed forces, the strain imposed by all this work was creating considerable problems which could not be addressed simply by recruiting female labour. Essential maintenance of the railways began to suffer as result. The situation had become so extreme by April 1916 that the Chairman of the Board of Trade was forced to write to the Railway Executive, stating:-

"If the railway service is impeded, or if any accident occurs owing to rolling stock getting out of condition in consequence of the railway workshops being engaged in the manufacture of munitions of war, I must hold the Railway Executive Committee responsible".

Such strong words were a severe indictment on the Executive, but secretly it must have come as a relief to many operating departments which faced the severest crisis in motive power and rolling stock availability in the history of railways.

The Executive could do nothing other

At the same company's carriage and wagon works at Newton Heath, Manchester, another type of urgent war production was undertaken. This was the construction of army lorries, in conjunction with the Leyland Motor Company. A variety of components for these motor lorries, including front axles, main frames, brake-compensating shafts, pedal shafts and gate changes were manufactured at Horwich Works. The components were assembled at Leyland, and then sent to Newton Heath for construction of bodies, cabs and cushions. The Government contract eventually calling for the works to supply 11 complete lorries per day.
NATIONAL RAILWAY MUSEUM

than comply with the wishes of the BoT, and stated that such work on munitions that was being carried on would only be done if it were not prejudicial to the safe running of the railways. However, it was found, that by now most of the machine work was being done by women and girls who, having learned the job thoroughly, were more suited to long repetitive orders than their male counterparts. The railway companies therefore continued to accept this work, but added that they must be allowed to refuse such orders as would delay the essential work on railway matters; and if they refused an order on these grounds, they would only take on such work on the receipt of a direct command from the BoT, who it turn would have to accept any consequences that might befall the railways as a result of vital maintenance being forsaken in preference to that for the military.

In the main, it was a marriage of convenience, and somehow the wishes of all the interested parties were met, this largely being at the expense of routine and non-essential maintenance, which was repeatedly deferred. In doing this, the railways were only postponing what they would inevitably have to face, and the Railway Executive made this point in no uncertain terms. In return the Government agreed to compensate the companies, and make good any losses they sustained by delaying their own work on behalf of the war effort. That is not to say railway maintenance did not take place in the war years, of course it did, though on a greatly reduced scale. Perhaps the greatest single indicator of the effect that war had on routine railway work, is the pathetically low number of new locomotives and stock turned out between 1915 and 1918.

Details pertaining to the activities of the different companies' non-railway activities during this period will be given in a future volume, but the following list of the railways involved in war work is of interest.

As the numbers of railway vans required for service overseas grew, it became evident that the ROD could no longer rely on the requisition of goods vehicles from the home railways. Accordingly, from late 1916 onwards, a series of specially designed 20-ton vans were ordered from a variety of workshops around the country. The view here shows the 'assembly line' production of vans at the LB&SCR's wagon works.

Barry
Brecon & Merthyr
Cambrian
Caledonian
Furness
Glasgow & Sth.
 Western
Great Central
Great Eastern
Great Northern
G.N. of Scotland
Great Western
Highland
Hull & Barnsley
Lancashire &
 Yorkshire
London & North Western

London & Sth.
 Western
London Brighton
 & Sth. Coast
Metropolitan
Meytropolitan District
Midland
Midland & GNR Joint
North British
North Eastern
North Staffordshire
Rhymney
South East & Chatham
Taff Vale
5 Irish railway works and
27 private railway
 workshops

The above list is not totally representative, for during the period concerned many other railway workshops were used for war-production, though in such cases the work was either of a limited quantity, or was undertaken sub-contract from another company. For example, the engineering facilities of the Maryport & Carlisle Railway were put at the disposal of the LNWR for a while, and later much work was undertaken there as sub-contract for Samuel Pearson & Co during their construction of the Gretna Munitions factory. However, whether a railway workshop was engaged in war-work or not, it can be safely said that all such facilities were worked to their maximum capacity during those troubled years.

Ambulance Trains

The value of ambulance trains was first recognised in the American Civil War, and their use in Atlanta, Georgia was portrayed in the epic film 'Gone with The Wind'. Britain's first such trains evolved in the South African War (1899-1902), when the British Red Cross Committee ordered the 'Princess Christian Hospital Train' from the Birmingham Railway, Carriage & Wagon Co., and had it shipped out to the Natal. Meanwhile, the War Office asked the L&SWR to adapt a five coach train to serve the wounded arriving back at Southampton. Impressed with its efficiency, the War Railway Council retained the L&SWR train and asked the LNWR to prepare plans for the conversion of ordinary bogie coaching stock into nine-coach ambulance trains: in turn the railway

An Ambulance Train being loaded at Doullens during the First World War
COPYRIGHT: IMPERIAL WAR MUSEUM. COURTESY: DR. BRIAN ROBERTSON

companies agreed to supply them in the following proportions: LNWR, three: GCR, GWR, and Midland two each; the GER, L&SWR and L&YR would each make one complete train.

When war broke out, all twelve were to be sent to Eastleigh to join the Red Cross and L&SWR ambulance trains, providing a total of fourteen such trains for use by the army. Correspondingly, the Royal Navy had none, as pre-war planning had centred largely on the use of hospital ships, and the large naval hospitals at Chatham, Portsmouth and Plymouth. The weaknesses in the Admiralty's planning soon became apparent, and on August 6th 1914 a request was sent to the LNWR carriage works at Wolverton to prepare five trains for the Navy in addition to those under construction for the Army.

The first wounded soldiers were landed at Southampton on August 24th, and because none of the new ambulance trains were yet available, it fell to using the old L&SWR train (supplemented with six coaches), in moving all

the injured to hospital at Netley. Later on that same day, the GCR train arrived and was immediately put to work. As hospitals around Southampton became over-crowded, the first ambulance train to take patients off the L&SWR system was No. 6 (supplied by the L&YR); on August 29th it transported 187 men to Well Hall Station on the South Eastern & Chatham. By 4 pm the following day, all twelve new trains were in use, but his was insufficient for the growing flow of the wounded, sick, and mental patients reaching Southampton and Dover. Four more trains were supplied in January, but meanwhile five emergency ambulance trains were formed to transport sitting cases. By February the allocation of the trains was: four ambulance, two emergency at Dover; and at Southampton; twelve ambulance, two emergency trains; the Red Cross train went to France, whilst the L&SWR set and one emergency train were allocated to the Navy.

By May 1915 the War Office intimated it needed more trains, for use both at home and overseas. To resolve how these needs could be

Ambulance train No. 29 on display prior to entering War Department service. These trains were somewhat smaller than the 16-coach continental ambulance trains, as the home trains could complete a round-trip to even the furthest destination inside 48 hours. Accordingly they did not require the same facilities as those used on the Continent where the trains might take several days to reach one of the channel ports used to repatriate the wounded.
M. ELTHAM COLLECTION

met, the Railway Executive formed two sub-committees, one for 'home' trains, and another for those needed on the continent. The home committee under H. Holmes (L&SWR), addressed the problem at once, and by the end of the war a total of twenty army ambulance trains had been supplied by just seven companies. A Continental Sub-committee was established under the chairmanship of F. H. Dent, of the South Eastern & Chatham. Along with H. D. Earl, Carriage Superintendent of the LNWR, and A. J. Hill, CME to the GER, Dent visited France to discuss the precise requirements with officials of the Surgeon-General's staff. Accordingly, designs were prepared for a standard train of sixteen vehicles, and in the years which followed British railway companies supplied a

total of 30 such trains for use by the British Army, in France, Egypt and Mesopotamia. A

Ambulance train 42 featured in 1917/18 along with the British and American nurses who manned these trains. The station has not been identified, but one of the nurses in the view was a relation of fellow railway historian Oliver Carter who would welcome more informationon the picture!
O. F. CARTER COLLECTION

further 19 ambulance trains were built for use by the American Army in France. In all, for British and American use overseas, the railway companies supplied a total of 822 ambulance coaches, of which only 30 were non-bogie stock.

Repatriated casualties were conveyed by ambulance trains to over 196 receiving stations, from where they were taken by road to hospitals near their homes, or those which had the special facilities to care for their injuries. Notification of ambulance train

Interior of train No. 37 showing one of the nine main cars. The three-tiered bunks show the numbers who might be conveyed thus, with the upper-bunks usually being reserved for the most serious cases. These bunks were never disturbed, but the two lower sets of bunks could be folded to provide comfortable seats on which the patients might lounge during the day. The idea of folding bunks/seats was instituted by the Railway Executive, but its design is attributed to F. W. Marillier, Carriage Manager of the GWR.

movements were often printed in the press, and at major railway stations it became practice for local people to bring gifts of food, flowers and newspapers for the wounded. Regretfully, many of the wounded died en-route, whilst others had to be removed to a hospital when the motion of the train opened up their wounds. The ambulance trains were treated with priority, but it was impossible to prevent them suffering problems which inevitably befall most railway movements. The most unfortunate incident was suffered by

men of the Northumberland Fusiliers and the Durham Light Infantry, on May 3rd 1915. While bound for hospital in Aberdeen, Train No. 9 became derailed just south of Kendal causing severe problems which necessitated at least one patient being removed to the Cumberland Infirmary in Carlisle. Generally, most of the workings arrived safely at their destination, and by the end of the war over five million soldiers, sailors and airmen had been conveyed by train to various hospitals in Britain.

By contrast the interiors of naval ambulance trains were considerably different, as the Navy preferred the use of folding canvas cots to stretchers. These were much easier to negotiate around the narrow passages and companion-ways of HM ships, and could be lifted vertically (as though the patient were standing) through hatches – particularly those on submarines. Once placed in a cot, the patient would normally remain cocooned within until he reached hospital. On the hospital trains, these cots were suspended from the roof by a series of tier brackets.

Demobilisation

As the war ground remorselessly on through 1917, and in spite of the continued movement of men to the 'front', the Railway Executive began to make plans for the eventual demobilisation of the troops. Though these plans were purely anticipatory, it seemed that following the American involvement, the allies would surely win – it was all a question of how long Germany would hold out.

The Executive Committee's plans were made personally by a group of General Managers, in recognition of the immense importance attached to the work by the War Office. The Committee had to address itself to a number of aspects of the demobilsation, which was split into two distinct parts – those men serving overseas, and those based at home. The War Office divided all its men into three categories, and by these groups they would be demobilised. First of these were the demobilisers; men who, in either military or civilian roles, would fill essential duties in the demobilisation of those who followed. Second were the 'Pivot-men'; men who would be employed in key occupations concerned with the reconstruction of Britain, a group in which coal miners, architects, builders, engineers and railwaymen were included. Finally, there came the demobilisation of 'other troops', including those of the Dominion forces.

Plans were drawn up to demobilise the troops through twenty Special Area Centres in

Troops disembark in the North-east in April 1919, having been conveyed there direct from Hamburg. The unit was to be sent to the large barracks at Catterick, and later disbanded as the men were sent to demobilisation centres around the country. In all this work, the railways played an important role, though from places like Newcastle, Hartlepool, Leith and Hull there was a considerable return traffic as the repatriation programme got underway.
KIRKLEES MUSEUMS & LIBRARIES

For the foreign soldiers who were left in Britain at the end of the war, repatriation was not as speedily instituted as they may have desired. Some countries were in such turmoil, it was impossible to return these men at once, as was the case with these Russian troops. Many were found useful work in Britain until the political situation in their own country settled down. As late as February 1920, such men were still waiting to go home but until then they were able to do useful work on the railways in north Northumberland.

NORTH OF ENGLAND OPEN AIR MUSEUM, BEAMISH

Britain, each centre representing a number of counties. Men who lived in, or intended to take up residence in those counties would be sent to that centre, regardless of which regiment or ship they had served in. For example, men from Cumberland, Lancashire, Westmorland and the Isle of Man would be sent to Area No. 3, for which the LNWR station at Prees Heath near Shrewsbury was the transportation point. Moving Home Command troops to the centres was considered to be a relatively easy task, but it was an entirely different situation concerning those overseas. Endeavouring to sort them out into the respective areas, and provide trains at the reception ports would be no small matter. The Executive reported its concerns to the War Office, and between them they envisaged a scheme which, as planned, promised an even sweeter operation than the mobilisation. Troops were to be sent to rest camps in France, each camp corresponding with a demobilisation centre in Britain. When

they were fully rested, and sufficient numbers had been collected, whole contingents would

Meanwhile not all of Britain's armed forces were allowed to return home, but even for those who were to remain in the services there were very generous leaves granted from the end of of 1918. Of the larger leave traffic, the bulk originated from naval depots in Scotland with Leith and Invergordon being the two principal centres from where men would head home. Ships were sent to one of the two establishments for re-fitting and the men would get up to a month's leave, and special trains were laid on for their benefit. The scene here at Invergordon station at the end of the year pictures one group of ratings who will be home for Christmas.

ROYAL NAVAL MUSEUM., PORTSMOUTH

be repatriated to the specified 'centre'. Where possible there would be through working from France to England, but it is not certain whether this would have involved the Richborough Train Ferry.

It was an admirably conceived scheme, and after the armistice it worked well for several weeks. Thereby about 20,000 men per day were returned from France, and along with 5-6,000 per day from British camps, they were conveyed to the area demobilisation centres. However, the transfer of men from camps in the Home Command was less orderly than had been anticipated. Each Area Command released about 500 men each day, issuing them all with a travel warrant. As there were no special travel arrangements for these men, the un-regulated flow caused considerable

difficulties for the railway companies who were unable to anticipate the demand for trains. In order to meet this situation, the Executive established 'railway assembly points' and demanded that, on release, all Home Command troops should first make their way to the one nearest their barracks. From these points, special trains were run on specific days of the week to the various centres, thereby moving the released men back to their home areas with the least possible inconvenience.

All went well with the front-line demobilisation, until the French authorities decided they could not tolerate the railway congestion imposed by sending men to rest camps for sorting. It announced that thereafter 'French Railways would only convey British troops to the nearest port' – a laughable fact when one considers that most of the French lines were only being worked thanks to the involvement of British railwaymen and locomotives. However, the War Office acceded to the demand, and thereafter the grouping of soldiers had to be done in England, with 'Area Centre trains' from the reception ports often being run in three or more parts to coincide with troop-ship arrivals. In this respect it

became necessary to run trains to each area camp from Tilbury, Southampton, Plymouth, Dover and ten other ports, so it is easy to appreciate how complicated the new arrangements came to be.

The demobilisation of the Colonial and Dominion forces was a different matter, for owing to the lack of available troop-ships, these men could not be repatriated to their home country immediately. Therefore they were established in camps near to their eventual embarkation points: Liverpool, Glasgow and

---

Unfortunately, not everyone returned as at least 16,000,000 men from all the countries involved lost their lives. The vast majority were buried in the great anonymous cemeteries of France, but some were returned for burial in their home towns. These men were usually those who died in hospital after being returned to Britain, or senior officers who were shipped back from France. The details of this Military Funeral at Dewsbury in 1918 are not recorded, though from the ceremony it might be assumed that it was either a senior officer or a soldier who had distinguished himself in battle.
KIRKLEES MUSEUMS & LIBRARIES

Avonmouth for the Canadians: Southampton for the Australians, New Zealanders and South Africans etc. In putting these men into camps, the Government felt it would like to allow as many of those who wanted, opportunity to see the motherland. Free warrants were issued, almost for unlimited travel, and various industries were instructed to welcome these 'colonials' and show them British methods of working. The railways were considerably helpful in this regard, and many of these soldiers underwent periods of training on British railways, in the hope that it might help them find jobs back home. Others, studied British transport methods with an eye to improving arrangements in their own industries. Fishermen from Newfoundland went to Peterhead and Aberdeen, to witness methods employed in the Scottish industry. South African fruit farmers went to Covent Garden to look at the market there, then they looked at steam heated railway vans with a view to using these to import their crops to Britain. It was much the same with sheep farmers from Australia and New Zealand who envisaged the use of refrigerated ships and railways in the supply of meat for Smithfield. In all these regards the railway companies cooperated fully, and nurtured the first seeds of what grew into a valuable import trade.

As far as the railways were concerned, demobilisation began on December 9th 1918. From here-on, the companies handled everything from men to machines, and from horses to tanks. On behalf of the War Office, they even accepted returned great-coats which could be handed in for a £1 gratuity at any railway station. By May 1919 only six of the Area Camps were left open; namely, Aldershot, Crystal Palace, Fovant, Prees Heath, Purfleet and Ripon. At the start of the following year Purfleet was the only one remaining, though Prees Heath and Fovant were converted into rest camps for men returning from overseas via Southampton, Plymouth and Liverpool docks. And so, our glimpse into the role of Britain's railways in World War One draws to an end. Much has been left unsaid, and much, much more is left to recounted. In future volumes we may look in more depth at some of the topics only briefly mentioned, but as always we need your help. If you have any recollections or photographs from this period, please do not hesitate to get in touch.